THE **COMPLETE IDIOT'S GUIDE** TO

Modern Manners

FAST-TRACK

by Mary M. Mitchell with Jim Weber

ALPHA
A member of Penguin Group (USA) Inc.

To Letitia Baldrige
I could not have asked for a better mentor or friend.

ALPHA BOOKS

Published by Penguin Group (USA) Inc.

Penguin Group (USA) Inc., 375 Hudson Street, New York, New York 10014, USA • Penguin Group (Canada), 90 Eglinton Avenue East, Suite 700, Toronto, Ontario M4P 2Y3, Canada (a division of Pearson Penguin Canada Inc.) • Penguin Books Ltd., 80 Strand, London WC2R 0RL, England • Penguin Ireland, 25 St. Stephen's Green, Dublin 2, Ireland (a division of Penguin Books Ltd.) • Penguin Group (Australia), 250 Camberwell Road, Camberwell, Victoria 3124, Australia (a division of Pearson Australia Group Pty. Ltd.) • Penguin Books India Pvt. Ltd., 11 Community Centre, Panchsheel Park, New Delhi—110 017, India • Penguin Group (NZ), 67 Apollo Drive, Rosedale, North Shore, Auckland 1311, New Zealand (a division of Pearson New Zealand Ltd.) • Penguin Books (South Africa) (Pty.) Ltd., 24 Sturdee Avenue, Rosebank, Johannesburg 2196, South Africa • Penguin Books Ltd., Registered Offices: 80 Strand, London WC2R 0RL, England

Copyright © 2013 by Mary M. Mitchell and Jim Weber

International Standard Book Number: 978-1-61564-232-8
Library of Congress Catalog Card Number: 2012912823

15   14   13   8   7   6   5   4   3   2   1

Interpretation of the printing code: The rightmost number of the first series of numbers is the year of the book's printing; the rightmost number of the second series of numbers is the number of the book's printing. For example, a printing code of 13-1 shows that the first printing occurred in 2013.

Printed in the United States of America

Note: This publication contains the opinions and ideas of its authors. It is intended to provide helpful and informative material on the subject matter covered. It is sold with the understanding that the authors and publisher are not engaged in rendering professional services in the book. If the reader requires personal assistance or advice, a competent professional should be consulted.

The authors and publisher specifically disclaim any responsibility for any liability, loss, or risk, personal or otherwise, which is incurred as a consequence, directly or indirectly, of the use and application of any of the contents of this book.

Most Alpha books are available at special quantity discounts for bulk purchases for sales promotions, premiums, fund-raising, or educational use. Special books, or book excerpts, can also be created to fit specific needs. For details, write: Special Markets, Alpha Books, 375 Hudson Street, New York, NY 10014.

Publisher: *Mike Sanders*

Executive Managing Editor: *Billy Fields*

Executive Acquisitions Editor: *Lori Cates Hand*

Development Editors: *Mark Reddin,*
Michael Thomas

Senior Production Editor: *Kayla Dugger*

Copy Editor: *Amy Borrelli*

Cover Designer: *Kurt Owens*

Book Designers: *William Thomas,*
Rebecca Batchelor

Indexer: *Angie Bess Martin*

Layout: *Brian Massey*

Proofreader: *John Etchison*

Contents

Introduction

We're only as successful as our weakest relationship. How we're able to connect with each other—whether in our jobs or our personal lives—dictates how effective we are. Nobody is perfect. We all mess up. Yet our ability to grease life's skids with a sincere "please," "thank you," "excuse me," and "I apologize" goes a long way to nurture relationships and set good examples for others.

Manners and etiquette are two different things. Manners—good manners—come from inside us. It's all about kindness and respect, both for oneself and also for others. Having good manners means having an attitude of mutual cooperation and civility. On the other hand, etiquette is a set of rules, the do's and don'ts of given situations that help avert chaos. Good manners give etiquette its authority. But whether we're talking about manners or etiquette, the bottom line in every interaction is to do what's kind.

As all of us experience the stress of difficult political and economic times, we're becoming more self-involved, thoughtless, inconsiderate, and rude. It happens without our even being aware of it, and surely not by intention.

This book is a reminder for even the most time-crunched of us to put ourselves in the other guy's shoes in the interests of smoother coexistence. Good manners and basic etiquette are democratizing factors, and they never were more useful than they are right now.

How This Book Is Organized

As a "fast-track" to modern manners, this book isn't meant to be a complete reference for all aspects of good manners. Rather, it's an on-the-spot, go-to handbook for the more common situations that present themselves in day-to-day living.

"You never get a second chance to make a first impression." This is the underlying premise on which **Chapter 1** is organized. First impressions are not only made face-to-face, but also through the telephone, the internet, and on paper.

Table manners continue to be a litmus test in both our personal and professional lives, as you'll see from reading **Chapter 2.**

Although the family of today may look very different from that of our grandparents, home is still very much where the heart is. Home is where we learn the most fundamental lessons, which are covered in **Chapter 3.**

Neighborhood issues can bring out the best and worst in us. **Chapter 4** is full of suggestions for neighborly living.

The lines between personal and work life blur increasingly, and **Chapter 5** will help you navigate the office and your business relationships.

Miraculous advances in technology give us new challenges for effectively dealing with each other. **Chapter 6** sets out guidelines for being savvy yet sensitive in cyberspace.

Handwritten messages carry more of an impact than ever, providing an opportunity to set ourselves apart in a truly positive light, as you will see in **Chapter 7.**

Learning how to be effective and constructive when face-to-face with others is what **Chapter 8** is all about.

Chapter 9 takes us on the road, with directions to help make the most of our travel experiences.

The curtain goes up on appropriate behavior, and it's time for lights, camera, and action in **Chapter 10** when out on the town.

Some of our biggest challenges and opportunities for growth come from interactions with those who are disabled. **Chapter 11** gives us perspective.

Occasions and celebrations represent transitions through the various phases of life. **Chapter 12** tells us what to expect and how to behave.

While time and attention are truly our most authentic gifts, they often translate into tangibles. **Chapter 13** details thoughts for gift-giving success.

Extras

You'll find sidebars throughout the book—brief, bright ideas that point out shortcuts and cautions along the way.

BONUS POINTS

These sidebars provide suggestions for observing courtesy in special circumstances.

MISERABLE MOMENTS

These sidebars point out potential pitfalls to help you avoid an unwarranted and detrimental faux pas.

Acknowledgments

This book would not have been possible without the support and guidance of my agent, Marilyn Allen, and acquisitions editor Lori Hand.

Additionally, the authors are grateful to the following for their helpful suggestions: Amy Abernathy, Letitia Baldrige, Frank Catalano, David Mason Eichman, Tyler Erickson, Jonathan Kremer, Penny LeGate, Karen Peterson, Dan Rudasill, and Johanna Karen Weber.

Trademarks

All terms mentioned in this book that are known to be or are suspected of being trademarks or service marks have been appropriately capitalized. Alpha Books and Penguin Group (USA) Inc. cannot attest to the accuracy of this information. Use of a term in this book should not be regarded as affecting the validity of any trademark or service mark.

First Impressions

First impressions often are as shallow as rainwater on a leaky roof. Yet they're as permanent as concrete, and if you're like most people, it would take at least a crowbar or an act of God to change them. Remember that perceptions are neither fair nor unfair. They simply exist. They can make or break a budding relationship. And though we live in an age of technology, we can't afford to forget that our relationships form the foundation of our lives.

Receiving a positive first impression is an uncomplicated experience. On the other hand, giving a first impression—one that's positive—can be very complicated. Awareness is key.

People think primarily of face-to-face meetings when they think about first impressions. What about the rest? What about first impressions on the telephone and in cyberspace, as well as on paper?

Never forget that people respond to how you make them feel. ⟲
A good first impression makes a person feel good about himself,
and by extension, feel good about you.

Face-to-Face Interactions

The first time you meet someone, you step into a bright and
unforgiving spotlight. Everything about you is intensified and
exaggerated—your manner, gestures, voice, facial expressions,
and what you wear (or don't wear).

What People See

What people see is critical. There's no such thing as neutral
clothing. Everything you wear represents a choice you've made
about how you want to be perceived. The bald truth is what they
see is what you get. If you look like a lowbrow, people will treat
you that way. And yet, a standard dress-for-success uniform is no
guarantee, either—fashion and good taste aren't necessarily syn-
onymous. Smart people dress appropriately for specific situations
and occasions.

The best way to figure out what to wear is to ask yourself who
you are, and how you want to be perceived. We all play different
roles in daily life. Is your role of the moment a soccer coach?
Student? Professional? Job applicant? Figure it out, and dress
that way.

Ask yourself where you are, and who are the people you want
to impress favorably. This isn't about making your own fashion
statement. It's about thinking through how the other person will
see you, filtered through the lens of that person's experiences—
job, generation, gender, geography, culture, etc.

If you don't know what to wear, ask! That's what human resource
directors, friends, hosts, and families are for.

"When in doubt, don't" is a pretty good guideline. Generally,
this rule applies in the workplace when it comes to spandex, tank
tops, sockless feet, and anything you would wear to the beach,

gym, or to clean out the garage. This guideline also works for extensive piercings, obvious tattoos, or showing excessive skin. Does this mean you shouldn't be authentic? Certainly not! It simply means you should minimize your risk of being unfairly, negatively judged until you're sure that your personal tastes won't become a barrier to critical relationships. That might mean compromise. As Coco Chanel famously said, "Be a caterpillar by day and a butterfly by night."

BONUS POINTS

Even though piercings and tattoos are becoming more and more prevalent, lots of workplaces don't consider them professional. It's prudent to cover up the tats and take the studs out of the tongue, eyebrow, nose, or any other unconventional place where they might attract attention when embarking on new job opportunities.

Unquestionably, we judge others on the basis of what we see more than any other single factor. And your mother and grandmother were right when they told you to stand up straight. Our posture is a clear indicator of our self-esteem. Once past the posture, people zero in on smile, hair, and skin.

That's where grooming comes in. Not everybody can have a perfectly formed smile of pearly white teeth. Still, everyone can have a clean smile, and everyone should work at that. Hair needs to be clean, styled, and not distracting because you must spend an inordinate amount of energy brushing it out of your eyes. Skin needs to be clean and fresh looking. Too much or too little makeup can be distracting. Finally, personal hygiene can't be overemphasized. Bathe or shower before your interaction. Brush your teeth. Use deodorant. Clean your fingernails and toenails, and don't even think about picking at your nails or teeth in public. Go easy on scents, whether they're perfumes, aftershaves, or hair products. A lot of people have allergies (or are simply sensitive to strong odors), and it's pretty embarrassing to cause an interviewer to sneeze, become teary, and cough when you're applying for a job.

Whatever you choose to wear, see that it's in good condition, clean, and fits you. When in doubt, see a tailor to finesse your garments' details—shoulders, chest, collar, lapels, armholes, and sleeves for shirts and jackets. Make sure that trousers or skirts are of appropriate length and in proportion to the rest of your outfit. Keep your shoes in good repair. Studies tell us that scuffed, dirty shoes suggest that a person pays no attention to detail, and that one's shoes are a good indicator of work performance.

Shaking Hands

In the United States, when we meet someone for the first time, the other person expects three nonverbal cues: a smile, eye contact, and a handshake.

BONUS POINTS

Always rise to the occasion and stand to shake hands. If you offer your hand while seated, unless you're the Queen of England, you appear to have no authority and no confidence. Even worse, you could come across as lazy or arrogant (as if to say, "It's not worth my trouble to stand up for this person").

It's easy to get so caught up in thinking about what to say that we forget to smile. A smile is one of the few universally understood gestures—so use it! Your smile can completely alter the atmosphere.

Eye contact can be challenging. If you're uncomfortable making eye contact, try this: instead of looking into someone's eyes, look at the space between his eyebrows. He won't be able to tell the difference. Eventually you'll work your way into the real thing.

Handshakes are a bit more difficult. People judge you by your handshake, so be sure that yours is firm and willing. The idea is to lock thumbs, so that you connect soft tissue to soft tissue, the "web" between the index finger and thumb. Shake firmly one or two times from the elbow. Remember, whoever gets the hand extended first controls the interchange. It's subtle yet true. To make a good impression, shake hands like you mean it.

 MISERABLE MOMENTS

Avoid shaking hands if your hand is soiled. Maybe you just ate some messy food. Say something like, "You wouldn't want to shake my hand right now," and get a napkin to clean your fingers.

Perhaps you have a skin condition such as a poison ivy reaction, or an injury to your right hand. Tie a scarf over the hand in that case, or bandage it, to indicate that it's out of commission. If your right hand is afflicted, extend your left hand to shake.

Good manners mandate that we never shake hands with gloves on, whether indoors or outside. Until the liberated 1960s, it was not customary for a gentleman to extend his hand first to a lady. But that was based on a code of chivalry that has given way to a gender-neutral approach to handshaking.

If you have a bad cold, say something like, "Forgive me for not shaking. I don't want to give you my cold." Never refuse a handshake, though. If someone with a cold offers you a hand to shake, go ahead and then, at the first opportunity, head for the washroom or hand sanitizer. It's not a bad idea to carry hand sanitizer with you!

Introducing Yourself and Others

Sooner or later you'll have to say something. Never be shy about introducing yourself, even when you might have been introduced previously. In many situations, it's absolutely necessary. Introduce yourself when you're at a gathering and you don't know the others.

When someone seems to remember you but is unable to place you, say something like, "We met at the flower show last year. I remember you were especially interested in the Japanese gardens."

You'll also want to introduce yourself when seated next to a stranger at a meal, or if the person expected to make the introductions fails to do so. All it takes is, "Hello, I'm Johanna." Say your name clearly and slowly. Never give yourself a title. Use both your first and last name when in a more formal setting such as a business meeting. Then give a nugget of information about yourself. The idea is to give the other person something to talk about with you. The nugget of information might be how you know your host, or your reason for being there. For example, "I'm such a big fan of John Grisham's mysteries that I couldn't resist coming to hear him speak. I'm a lawyer, too."

If you can't understand how to pronounce someone's name, ask, "Would you say that again for me? I didn't get it right." That shows you care enough to get things right. And that's a plus.

When introducing two people who don't know each other, the simplest method is to say, "Jon, this is Emily." Then give a nugget of information about each one. Try this: "Emily Weber just flew in from Seattle to referee this swim meet. Jon Watling is president of the swim team's parents' association." The preceding principle applies: the idea is to give each person a conversation starter.

Introduce a person of lesser authority to a person of greater authority. The way to do this is to speak first to the more senior person, saying something like: "Mr. Hollensteiner, this is Malcolm Baldrige, who is the star on our club basketball team. Malcolm, Mr. Hollensteiner has been a basketball coach, probably since before you were born."

If you only remember a person's first name when making introductions, just use that. If you only remember a person's last name, good-naturedly exaggerate the introduction by saying, "Ah, if it isn't Mr. Vandegrift" in a mock-formal manner. It may happen that you only recall the name of one of the two people you're introducing. Turn to the person whose name you forgot and say, "This is Cathy Robbins." Most likely the other party will take the cue and introduce himself.

You might not recall the name of someone you've spoken with before. Simply offer the following, by way of apology: "Please tell me your name again. My brain just froze. I remember so well talking with you at the coffee shop." Remember, everyone has blanked on names. We forgive others for mistakes we've made ourselves. By going straight for the solution, you aren't embarrassing anyone over the problem.

There may be times when you don't know whether to call someone by his first name. When in doubt, don't. That's a pretty solid rule to live by, and it's especially true if someone outranks you in age or position. It's a sign of respect and an invitation for him to change the rules and request that you use a first name. If you're at a reception and everyone is a peer, use first names. If you're a young associate, call older people by their surnames.

What People Hear

The first time someone hears you speak, he will tend to associate certain personality traits with the way you sound. For example, a resonant baritone may convey dependability, whereas a flat, weak voice conveys blandness. The so-called little-girl voice is entirely counterproductive when you want to come off as confident and authoritative. Ditto for speed talking.

Listen to your voice. Tape yourself, preferably during a conversation. You may find the results sobering. Listen for and try to change nasal tones, thinness, raspy sounds, and other unattractive elements. Work to develop resonance without booming like a camp-meeting revivalist. However, no amount of vocal acuity will replace sincerity. This goes for telephone first impressions as well as in-person ones.

Whatever words you speak, know that vulgar language, bad grammar, ethnic slurs, and suggestive tones will only work against you. Most people are embarrassed by such behavior and judge you negatively, yet don't know how to handle it, so they appear to go along. Make no mistake: you're shooting yourself in the foot.

MISERABLE MOMENTS

Someone has just introduced you by the wrong name. Simply whisper your correct name into the introducer's ear. You don't want him to be embarrassed by hearing it from anybody else.

When the Initial Interaction Is Not in Person

These days, people are more and more likely to limit their direct interactions, in part because we have come to rely increasingly upon the internet. We are able to stay wherever we are while connecting with others all over the world, which allows us to be "alone together." This phenomenon was first facilitated via the telephone. On the other hand, in earlier times, letter writers were very conscious and quite formal about the impressions they were creating by their initial written words.

On Paper

First impressions still create lasting perceptions of you. So when writing a letter, be sure to use the nicest paper you can afford, and don't use a ballpoint pen. A rollerball or felt tip leaves a more authoritative impression. Paper is a sensual experience; the finer the quality, the better impression you'll make. Write out the person's full name and use Mr., Ms., or Dr. where appropriate.

Online

Remember that email is eternal. There's no need to be as formal as "Dear So-and-So," unless you're sending a business-related email (for instance, a résumé). However, always use a salutation and a closing. They might be something like, "Good morning," "Hello," and so forth. Make sure your subject line is clear and current. Edit, edit, edit for any mistakes, typos, or misspelled words. If you make reference in your email to an attachment, make certain that you have remembered to attach the file before pressing the "send" button. And don't trust spell checkers; they might correctly spell the wrong word.

On the Telephone

One major telephone tip: when you leave a voicemail message, state your name and telephone number slowly and clearly both at the start and the close of the message. To ensure that you're understood, pretend that you're writing your name and number in the air. That will slow down your speech pattern enough to head off the inevitable frustration on the part of a listener who can't understand you. It goes a long way to create a positive first impression.

When it comes to cell phones, the general rule is that the person to whom you're speaking takes precedence over an incoming caller. Switching back and forth leaves both callers feeling less important.

Twenty-First-Century Table Manners

There was a time, not so very long ago, when good table manners were taught at home. Those were the days when families gathered together for a sit-down meal. Most of the time these days we eat on the fly, microwave frozen dinners, or grab a sandwich during lunch break. No wonder that correct table manners are becoming a lost art. We now have a generation raised without learning the correct way to behave at the table, subsequently raising the next generation.

The other big problem is that those who know better—for instance, the human resources person taking you out for a meal (an interaction that's really not about the food itself, but rather an interview of sorts)—won't tell you that you're eating like a pig. Yet they'll take note, and your lack of good table manners may well cost you a job or a promotion.

Table Settings and Using Flatware

Let's start with the absolute basics. When confronting the formal table setting, "reading" from left to right, you should see the napkin, the salad fork, the main course fork, the dinner plate, the knife (with cutting edge of blade turned inward), and the soup spoon. Dessert spoons either are placed above the plate with the bowl of the spoon facing left, or they're brought to the table with the dessert. Sometimes coffee or teaspoons are found next to the soup spoon, but they're often served with the coffee or tea separately.

If you should find the table set up incorrectly—which is all too often the case these days—simply go with the flow. You know better, and you'll set the table accurately in your own home!

The bread plate should be on your left; glasses are on the right, water glass on the inside, wine glass on the outside. If you get confused about whose glass is whose or whose bread plate is whose, simply join index finger to thumb on both hands, extending your other three fingers straight out, sort of like making the "A-OK" sign. You'll see a "b" on the left; "b" is for bread. And you'll notice the right hand is configured as a "d," for drink. Another way to remember it is (reading left to right again) "BMW"—bread, meal, water/wine.

If the person on one side of you has started using your bread plate, or drinking from your glass, again make the necessary adjustment and accommodate the faux pas. Manners trump etiquette, and it's good manners not to make the person next to you feel inept.

The napkin gets put in the lap and doesn't belong back on the table until you're getting up to leave. Even if you have to excuse yourself during the meal, keep the napkin off the table and leave it on your seat. Use the napkin liberally during the meal, dabbing your lips or the corner of your mouth as needed. Don't wave the napkin around like a flag in the breeze. When finished with the meal, place the napkin back on the table, to the left of your place setting. But don't refold it; refolded napkins can land on an unsuspecting diner's lap, still unlaundered, by mistake. Make sure the napkin looks like a napkin that has been used. A good rule is to make a circle with your thumb and index finger and run the napkin through it. The resulting shape tells the server your napkin goes in the laundry.

The knife always stays on the right, and only the right hand is used for cutting, even if you're left-handed. The left hand would be holding the fork to secure whatever you're cutting. Once a bite-sized portion has been cut off and the knife put down on the right side of the plate, bring the fork to your mouth with either hand, depending upon your hand dominance. Put the hand not being used in your lap until you're again ready to cut off another portion. Hold the fork (or the spoon) like a pencil rather than a garden tool; the index finger is used along the back of the blade of the knife to stabilize it while cutting.

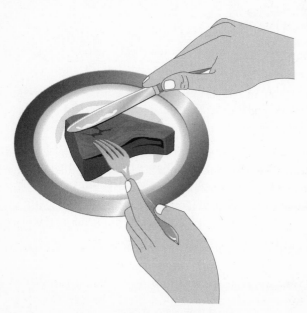

Knives and forks are held this way.

Table Manners 101

When attending a hosted meal, take your cues from the host. Don't sit until your host indicates where and when. Don't hesitate to stand when a guest enters the room to join you at table, or when a woman leaves or returns to the table. Don't be afraid to pull out the chair for a woman and help her seat herself. Chivalry is moribund, but not quite dead.

Don't order an appetizer or a drink unless the host encourages it. Feel free to decline alcohol, not in a pejorative way, but by saying something like, "Thank you, I'm not having wine today" (even if you never touch the stuff and disapprove of those who do). Using the word "today" removes judgment from your statement and contributes to the comfort of your fellow diner.

A few more don'ts:

- Don't slouch; remember that good posture is good manners.
- Don't season your food before you taste it. Often, especially in restaurants, there's already plenty of salt in the food.
- Don't feel you must polish off every single morsel on your plate.
- Don't talk with your mouth full.
- Don't put your handbag, briefcase, gloves, keys, eyeglasses, or cell phone on the dinner table. Anything not part of the meal has no place at the table, for reasons of hygiene as well as etiquette.
- Don't put your elbows on the table before the plates have been cleared away.

BONUS POINTS

If you practice eating politely at home, good manners will become ingrained. That way, you won't embarrass yourself when you go out. An even worse scenario would be for you to be an embarrassment to everyone around you without even realizing it!

When eating bread or a roll with the meal, use the bread plate if available. Break off a bite-sized portion. If you're using a spread, take some off the butter plate or out of the container and put it on the right side of your plate. Then spread whatever you need on your broken-off piece. Don't slather up the whole slice or half the roll before taking the first bite; butter each bite before you take it.

As you work down to the bottom of your soup bowl, it's fine to tilt the bowl, generally away from you, and direct the spoon from the center outward. Don't crumble crackers in your soup, tempting though it may be. And don't dunk. The spoon, when you finish the course, stays in the bowl if there is no plate underneath it. Leave the handle toward the right side of the bowl. If there's a plate under the bowl, leave the spoon on the right side of the plate.

Utensils used during the various courses of the meal never go back on the table. Nor are they to be left partly on the plate, partly on the table. If you aren't finished, but are pausing for conversation—always a good idea, unless you're at a silent retreat—put the utensils down in the shape of an upside-down "V." This is a silent signal to those few servers who have learned it. It simply means not to whisk your plate away because you're just resting and not finished with the course. Many waiters today will not have a clue! But you, at least, will know better. And you might even politely educate them, thus bringing back some modicum of correct table manners, one waiter at a time!

The signal that you're finished with the course is to line up your utensils, fork to the left and knife to the right, blade facing left, on the right side of your plate in a ten-to-four direction, as if the plate were the face of a nondigital clock. (Remember those?) Ditto when you're only using a fork or spoon. Having the handles angled off to the right makes it easier for the server to clear your plate from the right. Clearing plates from the right is the correct way to do it. Food is served, by the way, from the left.

Be sure you don't pick your teeth at the table. Ever. Nor, for that matter, should you apply lipstick. These actions you can do in the bathroom, or in the privacy of your car.

Difficult Foods, Preferences, and Intolerances

If you have allergies or other food intolerances, be sure to state them in a succinct and polite manner before ordering at a restaurant. If you're going to another's home for a meal, and the host has forgotten to ask, or you have had no opportunity to state your issues with food, eat whatever of the meal you can. If pressed as to why you're being so picky, simply say something with a tinge of self-deprecation, like, "I should have told you that peanuts land me in the ER." Be sure to follow that with "And don't worry; I didn't eat any."

BONUS POINTS

If your salad contains cherry tomatoes, think twice before eating them, unless they've been cut in half. There's virtually no way to eat one without running the risk of having it slip off your fork, bounce off the plate, plop into your lap, roll across the table, or splatter the person next to you. Eat the rest of your salad—and don't serve cherry tomatoes to your guests at home.

If you're vegan or vegetarian, and meat happens to make it to your plate, don't make comments about "road kill" or not wanting to "eat dead animals." Do the best you can. The key points here are communication and graciousness. It would not be rude to offer to bring a vegetarian dish to someone's dinner party.

BONUS POINTS

If you're given a steak that's well done, although you ordered it rare, you have a perfect right to ask the waiter to take the plate back; better yet, let the host, if present, do the asking for you.

On the other hand, if you ordered Indonesian curried tofu salad, having never had it before, and find that you don't like it, that would be your problem to muddle through.

Some Useful Caveats

No texting at the table. Period. Turn off the electronics and stow them out of sight.

If you're expecting a call that your third child has just been born far from where you unavoidably find yourself, explain the situation at the start of the meal and, with general acknowledgment (and a certain amount of wonderment), leave your phone on. If you get that call, immediately excuse yourself from the table. (Napkin stays on the chair; how quickly we forget!)

If you're hosting and a guest commits a faux pas, graciously do what you can to lessen their pain. There's the famous story, supposedly about Einstein's wife, who, seeing a finger bowl for the first time in her life, assumed that the contents were to be swallowed. She proceeded to lift the bowl and quaff the contents, flower and all. Her host, without hesitation, picked up his finger bowl and did the same, and, with a look around the table, clearly indicated that all guests were expected to do so as well. And they did!

MISERABLE MOMENTS

You have a nasty piece of gristle in your mouth. Don't surreptitiously spit it or any other inedible into your napkin. If you do, you may forget it's there and later, when you go to wipe your lips, drop it onto your new dress. Or worse, it might bounce across the table, which is guaranteed to stop all conversation. Quietly place the rejected item on one side of your plate without making a face or a big deal about it. Remove fish bones from your mouth with your fingers and put them on the side of your plate.

A reasonable guideline for tipping is 20 percent of the total bill, downscaled to 15 percent for service that isn't quite up to par. Restaurants will often automatically add the tip to the bill for groups of six or more, so be sure to look over the bill. Ask your server if you're uncertain. Remember to tip on the basis of the true amount of the bill if you're using a discount coupon.

It's perfectly reasonable to split the bill, and always reasonable to ask if you can pay for your meal. On the other hand, if you've invited someone out, you should expect to pay for them. Sometimes a nice compromise is to say "At least let me pay the tip."

Braving the Buffet

Buffets tend to bring out the worst in us. They tend to be confused with feeding troughs. Scope out the scene from a distance before you get on line. Where will you sit? Perhaps leave your jacket over the chair, or put your napkin on the seat of the chair. Then look to see whether there's one line or two, and where the utensils and trays are placed.

Don't cut in. There is, or should be, plenty of food for everybody. Don't pile your plate as high as you can, and don't take a heaping portion of shrimp if you see that there aren't many left for others. Don't go back for seconds until you're reasonably sure that everyone has had a first crack at the buffet.

Plates and utensils are generally reused at buffets in private homes, as well as all-you-can-eat restaurants. At an upscale restaurant, use fresh flatware and plates if you go back for more. Your servers will clear your place while you're going for seconds. Since people come and go throughout a buffet meal, it's unreasonable to stand each time this occurs.

The Modern
Home Front

The family of today can be considerably different from traditional representations. Same-sex parenting is becoming increasingly commonplace, especially with the growing acceptance of gay marriage and improvements in the success rates for artificial insemination. With continued immigration to our great melting pot of a nation, coupled with increased life expectancy and the rising costs of assisted living, comes the tendency toward keeping three and even four generations together under one roof. Adoption and foster parenting of children of different races and ethnicities and mixed-racial parenting are also more prevalent in today's society.

Most children have common sense; they know that being considerate, which is to say kind and respectful, is more likely to lead to smiles and hugs than being nasty. You'll want, as a parent, to keep reinforcing courteous behavior in your children.

Who Makes the Rules?

Parents make the rules; children break them. Punishment is meted out in many different ways. Obviously, disregard of a reasonable rule merits chastisement, and likely suspension of privileges. Some children are sensitive enough that a harsh word will suffice, while others disregard censuring and continue pushing the envelope to see just how much they can get away with.

This is not a book on proper parenting. But certain principles of manners must be emphasized. Perhaps first and foremost is that children aren't born inherently mannerly. Nor do they know anything about etiquette until they're taught. Again, being considerate, kind, and respectful is more likely to lead to smiles and hugs.

Parents or guardians need to be clear on house rules. There's no point in having a rule if the rule isn't clearly communicated. Understanding will be enhanced if the rule is stated and then discussed. Asking if you've been clear is a good idea. For instance, say, "Tell me what you just heard me say, so I'm clear that we understand each other." Asking whether the rule makes sense may be a bit more of a reach. And then asking if they understand you is a fool's errand, since by this point in time their eyes will be glazed over, and they'll nod in assent to just about anything.

BONUS POINTS

If you're a parent, you should set a good example of the behaviors you want to see from your children. After all, we teach and learn best by example. Nobody learns to ride a bike by reading how to do it. Which is not to say that you should disregard this book!

Children would rather run off and hang out with their peers than sit around and have to talk to adults, who almost seem like aliens. They'll want to veg out in front of the TV, or play Wii, or go on Facebook, or text their friends. They clearly, and more than ever today, prefer to be alone in their room. You'll need to encourage face time with you and your adult friends without seeming to force the issue.

Ask your child for his opinion about something in the news. Further, ask him what his friends think about that particular topic. Listen to what he says, and respond by validating; try, "What an interesting thought! That hadn't occurred to me."

Don't be overly rigid about things that don't really make that much difference; in other words, cut the kids some slack. Pick your battles; be as flexible as you can. And make kindness underlie your every action.

BONUS POINTS

Your son is told in no uncertain terms to be home by 10:00 by your husband, yet the concert doesn't even start until 9:00. Your child argues the point, to no avail. Although your son might be inclined to surreptitiously approach you, generally an easier mark, in hopes of getting a more lenient curfew, do not let him do so. Any attempt to set one parent against the other creates a losing scenario for everybody.

Wouldn't it be better for the family to have an unemotional discussion, where the son can present a logical reason for his position? Perhaps the compromise could be that he sees only the first half of the show in the interest of preserving family harmony.

Share the hard stuff with your spouse: don't set up a good cop/ bad cop situation. And don't try to be your child's best friend; that's not your role. Neither is it right to play favorites. Set a good example of the behaviors you want to see from your children.

Dealing with Divorce

If, as a parent, you're divorcing, make sure the children, however old they may be, understand that the divorce isn't their fault, and that both you and your ex-spouse will continue to love them and be available to them. Don't disparage your ex to the children, no matter how you really feel. Alienation of children from a parent is a terrible mistake. It will leave them far more scarred than they were already from the divorce itself. Never make your child a go-between, delivering messages, money, or anything else.

Getting Along with Your Blended Family

It worked for the Brady Bunch, but it might be a challenge for you. Children will resent any attempt that you as a stepparent may make to usurp their natural parent's role. On the other hand, children ultimately will respect your fair-minded authority in establishing house rules that apply to all.

As a new stepparent, you can take comfort from the fact that children will come to respect the harmony and support they see between you and their natural parent. Bite your tongue before speaking ill to the children of your spouse's ex. You will be respected and appreciated for that. An effort to be respectful and considerate will go a long way toward healing any breaches that may have developed. This would be true as well for dealings with stepsiblings.

Think before you blurt out something in anger that could adversely affect relationships for a long time. Be willing to shoulder the blame for something that didn't go well. Take a while to cool off; perceived slights seem to lessen in severity after a good night's sleep. Yet, if you can resolve differences before hitting the hay, everyone involved will be more likely to sleep better. Counting to 10 is more helpful than you might think. It works for both sides of any dispute, and is a very practical rule to live by.

There are times when a good, old-fashioned family meeting can be useful. Avoid two-against-one situations. Displaying good manners means letting the other person have his say, without being shouted down or interrupted. Avoid the accusatory "you"; use instead the first person, singular or plural. Be willing to compromise; a good compromise leaves both sides feeling that even though they didn't get everything they wanted, they got something. If a resolution is arrived at, plan to revisit the issue after a period of time to tweak things.

MISERABLE MOMENTS

A half-sister you never knew you had shows up unannounced at your house to meet the mother who gave her up for adoption. Practically every family has a few skeletons in the closet, but now the door has been opened, and the bones have come rattling out. Let's face it: this person has probably spent a great deal of time and likely money as well to get to your house. Let kindness and courtesy prevail, and things will work out.

It's generally better to try to keep family issues in the family, unless outside impartial mediation or intervention is warranted.

When Your Children Don't Look at All Like You

You may have adopted a child, or you and your spouse may be of a different race. Although neither situation ought to be problematic in today's more tolerant environment, classmates can be cruel and make unkind remarks. One would hope teachers would put a stop to such harassment. Yet teachers are often unaware that taunting like this is occurring. Without putting anyone on the defensive, tell the teacher, "Eleni is having a lot of trouble from classmates who call her names because she is a different color from her parents. Can you bring this issue up in class so that everybody learns?"

A family discussion would be in order here. Mixed racial and adoptive parents have to be prepared to deal with problems of this sort. The solution may be painful: the harassers may need to be disciplined, or the harassed child may need to be moved to another school. Yet the family unit should be strengthened through this type of adversity, and lessons in civility may be learned all around. One would hope issues like this will become less frequent in time.

As societal views regarding adoption evolve, the time-honored preference for confidentiality and secrecy is often being replaced with a degree of openness. Birth parents are increasingly having their say regarding the choice of the family who will adopt their child. More and more, birth parents are keeping in touch, either with the adopting parents or the child, or both.

If you're involved in a situation like this, expect times when all isn't smooth sailing. Any interaction with the birth parents may be awkward at best, contentious at worst. If you're the adopted child, you may harbor resentment toward your birth parents for giving you up. They may well have been wracked with guilt for many years. As hard as it might be, hold off before blaming your birth parents for abandonment. If you ever get to talk with your birth parent, try the fair-minded approach of asking: "Please help me to understand why you gave me up for adoption. It must have been hard for you, but it hasn't been easy for me, either." This should open the door to some healing discussion. If there are awkward silences, don't hesitate to say, "Please tell me more; I'll do my best to try to understand."

If you're an adoptive parent, you may have good reason to prefer that there be no contact with one or both of the birth parents, assuming that you know their identity. Yet your adopted child will reach a point in time when he's of age and legally able to make decisions regarding contact with one or both birth parents. Put yourself in his place: wouldn't you want to know where you came from?

Here again, a civil, respectful discussion will be helpful. Be prepared to compromise. At the very least, recognize that the child you adopted may want, and generally deserves, to know more about his birth history. Asking such questions doesn't mean that he doesn't love you and accept you as a parent.

It would be worthwhile at this point to tell your child about the many hurdles you had to jump over and the long months you had to wait until that final moment when the papers were signed and the adoption process completed—a moment every bit as charged with emotion as childbirth itself. Your child may still want to attempt to establish contact with his birth parents, but he'll now have things in a little better perspective.

Accommodations in the Multigenerational Family

If you live with several generations of family in your home, consider yourself lucky. You have at your hands the wisdom of great experience and the perspective of life in war and peace, in times of general prosperity and widespread despair. All you need to do is listen and take it all in. Having good manners means being patient and listening. Be patient with the elderly—they may not move or react as quickly as you; they likely can't see or hear with your acuity; their habits may seem out of touch with your modern ways; they're as rigid in their ways as they are in their bodies. Yet they have much they can teach you, if only you'll listen.

You may be in a position of having to care for an elderly relative, to make decisions for one who used to make decisions for you, perhaps for the whole family. Be respectful. It isn't easy to get on in age. As General Charles de Gaulle famously said, "Old age isn't for sissies." Treat the senior person the way you would hope to be treated in your turn. Set a good example for your children. Help the older generation feel more relevant.

Ask their advice about things, even when you feel you already know the answer. Make the effort to bring them into the conversation.

Ask them about their childhood, the remote family history, what it was like to live in the Old World, what their immigration experiences were like. Encourage them to assimilate; take them out and around with you. Be proud of your heritage and honor this living link with the past. Don't end up wishing you had found out more when it's too late to ask.

> **BONUS POINTS**
>
> When it comes to technology, accept certain generational differences:
>
> - Millennials (born after 1980) rarely stop long enough to listen to voicemails; they prefer texting to emails. They might even buy their groceries online.
> - Gen Xers (born between 1965 and 1980) may prefer either text or voicemail.
> - Baby boomers (born between 1946 and 1964) leave messages; it's a big improvement over the hours they used to spend on near-terminal hold. But some won't have the dexterity of thumbs to do a lot of fast texting.
> - The Greatest Generation (born before 1946) is still trying to figure out how all these newfangled things work anyway.

The fact is there are plenty of households today where four generations live together—great grandparents, grandparents, parents, and children. Communication can be tricky in such circumstances. Patience, respect, kindness, and courtesy are key words, if we are all to get along.

Same-Sex Parents: No Apologies, No Excuses

If your family features parents of the same gender, you have every right to expect the same courtesies and respect that are afforded to families of a more traditional nature.

Parenting or growing up in such an environment will present challenges, from inside the house and out. This isn't unique; all parents and all children face challenges. The key is what you make of these matters. Issues continue to come up, and they can either bring the family unit closer together, or they can contribute to fragmentation. Keep in mind that, when all is said and done, family needs to come first. And it makes no difference whether that family is traditional, blended, or the product of a gay relationship.

Expect the unexpected. Don't be surprised when you're the butt of cruel jokes and innuendoes. Keep your head high. Set a good example. Contribute to your community, whether it be socially, politically, economically, or culturally; the community will come to recognize what an asset you and your family are, and everyone will come out ahead. So what if there are a few bumps along the way?

The fact is, most of the staring you'll experience as part of a same-sex parent family has no malicious intent behind it. People are simply trying to figure out what's going on. A pleasant smile from your end of the sharing process will most likely open positive lines of silent communication, and all will be well.

Foster Families

Some of the biggest challenges to the cohesive family unit come from this situation. Bringing another child or a teen into an already existing household requires patience, cooperation, and compassion. Many foster children come from troubled backgrounds; their value system is askew. They need guidance. They challenge authority. They resent authority. They may have criminal records. As a considerate parent, you may need to say, "I don't understand why you are doing this. Please tell me more so that I can see where you're coming from." If this doesn't resolve the issue, seek out a foster parenting support group— perhaps also a social worker and a psychologist.

On the other hand, a foster child may well turn out to be the glue that holds a fragmenting family unit together. Rallying around the new kid in the house, who is really a long-term guest, can be a gratifying and validating experience for all.

A family meeting before the foster child arrives is essential. Family members deserve to know what they are getting into. Set up a tentative plan, assigning each family member a welcoming role. For example, one child might be delegated to showing the newcomer how to do the laundry, another the cleanup after meals. In about a week, convene another family meeting, including the new family addition, to reassign tasks.

Many foster children have never known what it's like to be loved, so show them love. At first, they'll find it hard to respond, but they'll come around. Give them the benefit of the doubt. Don't expect their natural reticence to disappear overnight. Keep trying. You may be saving a life.

Neighborly Ways

You've picked out your significant other and chosen the place in which you live. Unfortunately, you haven't been able to control the neighborhood. Certainly, you may have knocked on a few doors before inking the contract on your place, and the people you met may have seemed nice enough at the time. Of course, you may have caught them on a good day. Besides, the nice ones seem to move on, and you're never quite sure about the new ones who move in.

There will be some neighbors, perhaps even right next door, whom you've hardly ever seen, let alone spoken to. Perhaps they are shy or reclusive; perhaps they work the graveyard shift; perhaps they are hardly ever in town. And the desire for privacy always ought to be respected.

New Neighbors

If people move in next door, make an effort to welcome them. If you're the new neighbor and the community hasn't reached out to you, then reach out to them. Hold an open house; invite everybody. Some will not come, but all will hear about your friendliness, and those who missed out should be given a second chance to see how cool you are.

Bake a few cookies and go knock on the doors of those you haven't yet met. In other words, do everything you can to start off on the right foot. If you have that new person or family moving in, wouldn't you want to get to know them? Some may quickly give you the clear impression that a cursory introduction is about as far as they want to pursue the acquaintance. In such cases, back off gracefully and try not to take the rejection personally.

BONUS POINTS

Speaking of starting out on the wrong foot, if you're visiting some-one and see shoes lined up outside the door, assume that you're entering a home where shoes aren't worn inside. Do likewise and shed yours, even if your host says it's all right to keep them on. When in Rome, do as the Romans do—at least those who go shoe-less in their houses!

Perhaps things have been a little icy in the old neighborhood of late. That new family might just serve as an icebreaker. Before you know it, you'll be having block parties or pie bake-offs.

Certainly you'll want a new neighbor to know if there are certain special expectations to be met, such as no loud parties on the roof deck after 10 P.M., or collapsing empty cardboard boxes before putting them into the recycle bin. Having a set of rules (better to soften the term to "suggestions") for neighborly living in your community would be useful, especially if presented in a cheerful manner and not sent certified mail—return receipt requested.

On the other hand, if you are the new neighbor, you will want to know if there are some possibly idiosyncratic regulations. Even if they seem a bit far-fetched, you'll want to respect them, at least until you're in a position to influence others to modify them.

Helping Out

Being a good neighbor means helping out. Everyone can use a hand from time to time. Be cheerful in the way you make the offer, and don't take offense if your offer is declined.

Offer to bring in the mail if your neighbor is going out of town. Or if your neighbor has been ill, she may need a little extra help with the trash. Perhaps a casserole or a pot of soup in those first few days home from the hospital would help. Try simply asking if there's anything you can do.

The person you're offering help may not want to be beholden to others, but you can set her mind at ease on that score with a reassuring comment like: "You know, when I had my hip replaced and Jon was called away on an urgent business matter, I sure was glad when you brought over a few home-cooked meals. I simply would like to pay forward on that debt. Won't you consider letting me help out a bit, at least until you're feeling stronger? It's really no trouble." Wow! Who could refuse an offer like that?

Remember that coming around to be friendly or helpful is one thing. Snooping around or prying into matters that are none of your business is another. Be nice, not nosy.

Noise and Smelly Stuff

One of the worst ways to set your neighbor's teeth on edge is to interfere with her sleep. Music played too loud, with or without partying late into the night, is particularly irritating. Hopefully, the neighbor will be polite in her request that you tone it down. However, if you ignore her, don't be surprised to find a policeman knocking on your door.

Neighborly spats can easily escalate into full-scale war—witness the Hatfields and the McCoys (or the Montagues and the Capulets, for those of you who were English majors). Be the one to make that first peaceful overture. Swallow your pride and see what happens. It just might work!

BONUS POINTS

Turn the volume down on the late-night TV, especially if the windows are open. You can watch a movie on your computer, using earphones, and nobody will be disturbed. And remind the contractor not to show up with his work crews before 8 A.M. and to knock off by 5 P.M. We are talking the Golden Rule here, so be considerate.

Barbecues may be fun for you but an annoyance for your neighbors. If you live in close proximity and the prevailing winds are frequently in the direction of your neighbors, they might well object to all that smoke wafting through their living room windows on a warm summer's evening. Be considerate, and tell them that you're having some friends over. Move the grill, if feasible, or set up a screen. At the very least, apologize in advance for any inconvenience.

As for smoking, obviously what you choose to do in your house is your business. Just don't expect the neighbors who are sensitive to smoke allergens to relish coming over. And if you're visiting and would like to smoke, ask first and don't wear a long face if your request for permission is turned down (hopefully politely). No ashtrays in sight would be a major clue that you're in a no-smoking household. You can always excuse yourself and go outside for a few puffs. Say, "Can you direct me to the smoking area outside? I'll be right back." Avoid smoking right outside the screen door or under a window. Dispose of the cigarette butts in an ashtray or the garbage; don't leave them in the bushes or on the lawn.

A few special considerations for apartment and condo living:

- Respect common areas. Don't leave trash lying about. Be courteous on elevators. Observe no-smoking rules.

- Don't leave your clothes unattended in a shared laundry space; others will want to use the machines and counters, too.

- While respecting quiet hours, also remember that walls are often quite thin, and your neighbors may be trying to sleep during the day, if they work nights.

- Participate in recycling efforts that are good for the environment, as well as a way to keep trash bills down.

- Decorate your patio inoffensively.

- If you park in the building lot or garage, be sure to park within the lines that demarcate each space.

- Don't let people unknown to you enter your building or parking garage. Ask them politely yet firmly to contact the apartment manager.

- Avoid altercations; you never know whether the other person may be armed. If necessary, report suspicious people to the police.

Talking Trash

Odors from overstuffed garbage cans can get pretty offensive. Lately, cities are talking about picking up the trash every *other* week, so this situation may get a lot worse. You may have to make a few trips to the local waste station, if you end up on some occasions with more than your can will hold. Having a second garbage can for that occasional overflow would certainly help.

Leaving lots of junk around your place won't win you any positive points from the folks on your block. Yes indeed, your home is your castle, but your yard is not to be confused with the city dump. It can be tough to edit out some of your prize junk. But let's get real here: do you really need the rear axle from your grandfather's Buick?

If you let your front or back lawn go to weed, your lot will look trashy, whether or not it's filled with junk. If you're unable to care for the lawn, odds are the neighbors will offer to help, either because they're taking pity, or because they're afraid the value of their real estate will plummet. Whatever the reason, take them up on their offer. Or hire the neighborhood kid to take care of it for you. If your front and back yard are in decent shape, you'll feel better. That's a guarantee.

MISERABLE MOMENTS

Your beloved cherry tree continues to grow. Unfortunately, your next-door neighbor has gotten tired of asking you to trim it away from her property and has taken matters into her own hands. Now the tree looks misshapen to you, and you're furious. The fact is, the neighbor was within her rights. Head off such unpleasantness by trimming it yourself or by offering to clean up the leaves in her yard.

Pet Peeves

There are over 78 million pet dogs in the United States. Almost 40 percent of households have at least one dog. Estimates for cats run from 70 to 80 million. And these estimates don't include strays! Add to these numbers 16 million caged birds, and you have an average of one pet for every other person in the United States. So the odds are good that there are plenty of pets in your neighborhood.

Unless you live in a cooperative community or a building that prohibits animals, you have little or no control over the number of pets your neighbors have, or the way the animals behave. Cats are especially independent; they may pop into your place unannounced. While this may be a welcome event, it could also make things unpleasant if you're allergic to cat dander.

It can be quite a challenge to keep your cat from roaming, since it can squeeze through pretty small spaces and leap up on almost anything. It can also be tough to avoid the occasional cat fights, most of which seem to occur when animals go into heat. But this you must try to do, if you want to be a good neighbor.

Dogs are easier to fence in, but their barking and growling can be a nuisance, too. Proper attention to training, ideally right from puppyhood, should wipe out such problems, but professional intervention may be required, especially if you bring in an older dog to a new neighborhood.

Letting your dog out to nose about unattended in the neighborhood is bound to result in plenty of poop on the ground. If you're not right there to clean it up, it remains as a hazard or at least an irritant. Most cities have leash laws, and for good reason. A good dog guardian (a better term than "owner," really) will clean up random deposits, even if they aren't from her dog, in the interest of keeping the neighborhood clean.

Birds can be nuisances, too. Fortunately, covering their cage to quiet them down usually works.

The bottom line is that pet ownership and neighborliness can coexist. Pet owners need to be considerate, and neighbors need to be forgiving. Accidents will happen, but good manners carry the day.

BONUS POINTS

You've taken your dog out to do its business and left it plenty of food and water. An accident on the way home from work puts you in the emergency room. Your husband is visiting his mother in Florida. What about the poor dog? Fortunately you've stashed a key under a flowerpot. Or perhaps a friendly neighbor keeps a key to your place, just in case. Problem solved. Now, if you can just get out of that ER ....

Garage Sales

Garage sales can be fun events for your neighborhood—or a nuisance. Garage sales bring in all manner of interesting people, from the casual drop-in to the veteran bargain hunter and garage-sale addict. Some very colorful people will show up, and you may make a few new friends. You never know.

The event can be a way to bring your neighbors together. Everyone has belongings they don't need anymore, yet few people want to sit outside all weekend in hopes of selling a thing or two. So why not join with some neighbors to have a combined garage sale? That way, there will be a larger, more alluring variety of stuff on display, and the job of sitting there can be split into shifts. Heck, it might even be fun!

At the very least, if your family is going solo on the garage sale, consider "warning" your neighbors before you go plastering signs all over the place and attracting strangers into your formerly peaceful little corner of the world. And don't let the thing drag on for more than two days (all right, three, if it's a holiday weekend). Be grateful that people are paying you to haul away your junk.

But maybe you're the one thinking about leaving your own neighborhood to see if you can pick up something you can't live without for something less than you think it's really worth. In that case, here are a few suggestions for proper garage sale manners:

- Don't show up early and holler into the house, "Hey, are you selling a goldfish bowl, by any chance?"

- Park your car and walk to the sale. Don't cruise by and gawk from your car; you'll cause an accident sooner or later.

- Leave your dog at home or in the car. If you feel you must bring the pooch along, ask permission. Remember that if the dog soils something, you have just bought it.

- If you feel you must bring the kids along, be sure they behave themselves. Do not expect the garage sale host to entertain them. (Do not expect the garage sale host to entertain *you*, either.)
- Wear your glasses; asking "How much is this?" is tacky when the price is marked on the item.
- Don't ask to use the bathroom or borrow the phone.
- Show up with something less than a $50 bill in your handbag.
- Bargain if you must, but be respectful. Don't haggle over something marked 50 cents; preserve a little dignity.
- Thank the host as you leave, even if you didn't buy a thing.

Sellers and potential buyers alike have a real opportunity at garage sales to demonstrate or develop proficiency in respectfulness, generosity, and gratitude. The experience is, or at least can be, worthwhile.

Manners at Work

Put more than one person in a room together, and you need rules to get along, especially in today's workplace, with cubicle environments and a wide age range of employees, all expected to collaborate constructively. We all can, and should, do our bit by pitching in to evade the potential blowups. Good manners create good relationships. Good relationships create good business. It's not the other way around. (Hasn't somebody famous said this before?)

Business manners are based on rank. The biggest star gets top billing, regardless of gender. Whoever needs the help gets the help, regardless of gender. Thus, women open doors for men when it makes sense, and vice versa. Is chivalry dead in today's workplace? Not necessarily. If a man chooses to pull out a chair for a woman, or to open a door for her, she should be secure enough to accept the kindness graciously. The tipping point is that women, who by law receive equal pay for equal work, don't have the right to expect to have doors opened and chairs pulled out for them anymore.

BONUS POINTS

Most important, remember that "please," "thank you," and "excuse me" are gender neutral and always appropriate, regardless of your place in the pecking order. In fact, the higher up the ladder you are, the better your manners should be. How else will anybody learn from you?

Just because we happen to be having a tough day doesn't give us license to take it out on anybody else. That's why negative attitudes—such as surliness, being late, and general unpleasantness—are the number one business behavior mistake we can make. Our words and actions have an effect on others. No one's life is exempt from stress or frustration; they're guaranteed, just like death and taxes.

With a slightly better attitude, the same "nasty" people might find support and sympathy for whatever is upsetting them. But by being rude, they're just making matters worse for themselves and everyone around them. At best, nasty people are distancing themselves from a solution. At worst, they're jeopardizing their career. And all of this reflects right back to the top of the organization.

Cubicle Etiquette

Too many people, so little pricey office space; thus, we have the cubicle office. Turf wars abound, and for some good reasons. We all need some space to call our own, however limited it might be. Yet when it's our office, and we're collecting a paycheck, we've bought into the organization's brand and vision. That means we need to make sure that our space is orderly looking, and that whatever memorabilia we choose to display is in good taste and within the company's visual bounds.

While it's tempting just to barge into your co-worker's cubicle, beware! Your enthusiasm will be misinterpreted as an invasion of privacy, however public that private space might seem. The fact is, privacy becomes all the more precious because there's so little of it in cubicle complexes.

In the interest of constructive colleagueship, stand at the cubicle's entrance and ask if the person has time to speak with you. You might not even need to enter the cubicle at all if the matter is something minor and can be handled quickly.

MISERABLE MOMENTS

Your son has gotten into trouble at school and the principal has phoned you at work. While you're talking with him, your supervisor barges in. He's always in a rush, and used to giving the orders. Remember that your cubicle is your space, excuse yourself to the principal, cover the speaker of your phone with your hand, and politely yet firmly inform your boss that you're on an emergency call and will stop by his cubicle as soon as you can.

Hanging over the cubicle partitions definitely isn't respecting the other person's space, even though you're not actually entering it. Never drape yourself over the top of the partition, and never, ever peer over to see what the other guy is doing. Pretend that there are real walls separating you, and behave that way.

Remember that these imaginary walls are also very, very thin. So thin, in fact, that your neighbors can hear what you're saying on the phone unless you modulate down to *sotto voce* (lowered voice). And speaking of *sotto voce*, never listen to voicemail messages on speaker phone. Conduct personal business on your cell phone or on a phone in an empty conference room or alcove whenever possible.

Equally importantly, remember that your pepperoni pizza can be smelled by others—and incessantly tapping your foot on the floor can be felt as well.

Even though cubicles allow easy access, and whatever supplies inside them are company property, don't ever "borrow" something from your neighbor without permission. Need a pen or some paper? Go to the supply closet. Don't even think about accessing your neighbor's computer without permission.

Food in the Office

Lunch or a snack at your desk? It's rude to eat in front of someone else, but nobody expects you to share your Philly cheese steak should they walk in on you. Unless you want the other person to sit down, stand up and ask if you can get back to him when you're finished. Give a time frame, and stick to it. Try, "I'll be finished in another 10 minutes and will come by then."

The caveat here is that your lunch shouldn't smell and thus attract attention, negative or positive. It's not bait for a visit. Nobody should be able to hear you chomping on crunchy potato chips, either, or slurping your soup or your beverage. Otherwise, you'll end up the brunt of office jokes, and deservedly so.

When the office has a communal kitchen, some rules apply. The first rule is to have some rules that spell out who's in charge of the kitchen, and when and how it's cleaned. Post the rules clearly, together with whatever rule you might have about kitchen postings. Is the refrigerator door fair game for announcements beyond the cleaning schedule? If it's off limits, let everybody know as much.

Refrigerators need to be cleaned out every week, and food shouldn't be stored there over weekends. Never bring smelly food to the fridge in the first place. Whatever you bring, make sure it's in airtight containers and that you label the containers with your name. Unlabeled food isn't necessarily an invitation to scarf it down. When in doubt, ask. Better still, if you're bringing something in for the entire department to enjoy, put a note on it and say so. And don't be a space hog, monopolizing the fridge with a container that's flattening everybody else's focaccia. Make sure to close the refrigerator door.

MISERABLE MOMENTS

Did someone steal your lunch? If it was clearly labeled, then ask around without making a fuss. Give the culprit the benefit of the doubt—this time. Mention it to your department head so that it can be brought up at the next office meeting. You also could send an interoffice email or text with a little humor (at least at first), offering a reward to the person who brings it back, no questions asked.

Microwaves are not for cooking at the office. They're only for heating food, so don't monopolize them, and don't walk away and leave them while something of yours is being heated. Be careful what you prepare so that your food doesn't leave the entire office redolent of *eau de popcorn*, or worse. In fact, some offices have rules against popcorn because of the smell and also the likelihood of setting off the smoke alarm.

Many offices use single-serving coffeemakers. While this eliminates the hassle of who cleans the coffeepot, it still means that whoever drinks last cleans up after himself and gets the machine ready for the next person. So dispose of the used container, and be sure to wipe up any drips. If your office has a regular coffee pot, the same consideration applies.

The Boy Scout rule to leave the campsite cleaner than you found it is a worthy rule for office kitchen sinks and counters. Crumbs have no place on counters or in the sink. Wash your own mug, plate, silverware, and glasses, and put them in the drainer right away. No fair leaving dirty dishes in the sink. If it didn't work with your mother, you can be sure it won't fly with your co-workers.

Whether it's your desk, the office refrigerator, the coffeepot, the counter, the sink, or the floor—if you spill something, clean it up. Your colleagues aren't your servants, just as you aren't theirs.

Doors, Elevators, and Escalators

Unless you were hired as a doorman, there's no need to hold the door for everyone in sight. If you see someone coming along with arms filled with packages, files, or whatever, by all means open the door for him. And of course, if someone on crutches or in a wheelchair is approaching, help out. Remember the basic rule—whoever needs the help, gets the help, regardless of gender. Most of us can open our own doors. However, if you're with a senior executive or honored guest, it's best to let that person reach the door and go ahead of you.

Elevators magnify the pressures of limited space. If you're among the first to enter on the ground floor and will be getting off at one of the lower floors, stand in the corner near the door and let others fill in the space behind you. If you're in the front and are getting off at a higher floor, step out at intervening stops, hold your hand on the door to prevent it from closing, and reboard after others have gotten off. If you're at the control panel, press the hold button to keep the doors open until everyone is aboard; then ask people to call out their floors so that you can press the floor buttons for them.

Once inside, don't remove hats, coats, or gloves; you may bump others or cause them to think you will. Mind that you don't whack others with your backpack or yoga bag. Make eye contact, smile, and say hello if you want to. Think twice before engaging in conversation; you never know who's listening.

The escalator mantra is "keep moving." Look where you're stepping when you get on, so you have sure footing. Stick to the right and hold on to the rails so that passengers in a hurry can get around you on the left. Here again, don't engage in conversation with the person on the step above or below you. Sound carries, and you never know who might hear your opinions of office issues, or worse, people. Once you reach the top, move quickly out of the way to avoid a pileup of passengers behind you. The escalator is no place to daydream.

Office Parties

You can't take the "office" out of the office party. Office parties are unbeatable opportunities to meet co-workers under different circumstances. Otherwise, you might not get to meet the company CEO or people in different departments. With some preparation and forethought, you can show yourself in your best light and also bring out the best in others.

Barring some extreme situations such as hospitalization or a death in the family, accepting the invitation is non-negotiable. Do that as soon as you receive the invitation. Your invitation will indicate if it's okay to bring a date or a spouse. Generally, if the invitation does not specify "and guest," it means that you go solo.

Once you accept the invitation—and not before—it's fine to ask who else will be there. Should someone question you on that point, say, "I want to be sure to look out for people whose names are familiar but I've never met." You'll know by the invitation whether the party is casual or more formal. If it's not clear, ask whoever invited you or the human resources department for guidance. Once you get an idea of what the setting will be, make sure that whatever you decide to wear doesn't show too much skin or too many tattoos or piercings, and isn't too tight or too short.

Even though you might not be enthusiastic about going to your office party, arrive no later than 30 minutes after the start time. Leave at or a little before the stated closing time. No fair breezing in shortly before the end to make a cameo appearance just because you really don't want to go. No fair leaving too early. Your inappropriate arrival and departure times will be noticed.

Ear buds are not an appropriate office party accessory; neither are smartphones or any other kind of phone. You're there to make new relationships and nurture ones you already have. Spend your time focusing on others. You can't do that if you, in effect, retain your connection to cyberspace while at the party.

Office parties are no time for "talking shop." The idea is to engage others in conversations you wouldn't have on the job, especially if you don't know them. Part of your preparation should include thinking about topics to talk about. Movies, sports, music—what you might have seen and heard on television or radio—are all fair game. Ask others what they do for fun when they're not working, for example. You might discover that you share common interests.

BONUS POINTS

Never go to any business social event hungry. You're not there for the food. Snack on something before you arrive so that you won't drool the minute you enter the room, or worse, get loopy on a sniff of wine. Go easy on the alcohol altogether. For one thing, moderation could prevent you from making a fool of yourself, and for another, your overconsumption will be duly noted by the powers that be. It could be tough to live that down.

Don't try to carry both a plate and a glass. Take one or the other, and carry it in your left hand, leaving the right one clean, warm, and dry to shake hands. Put only a very few hors d'oeuvres on your plate, and if they're passed, take only one at a time.

Remember that everyone has an agenda at a business or social event. To break free from someone who's monopolizing you, it's okay to say, "I'm glad we had a chance to talk a bit. If you'll excuse me, there are a couple of people I really want to catch up with before the party ends." Should any of your conversations warrant a follow-up, make sure you do that. For example, if you mention information useful to someone, send along the information link or whatever would be helpful. That simple action will set you apart as someone who's thoughtful, helpful, follows through, and above all, truly listens.

Never forget that we judge others more based on what we see than any other single factor. So by all means be festive, but not foolish. Watch your body language—kissing and hugging, regardless of how innocent, are just not in your best interest.

Before you leave, thank your host in person, without monopolizing his time. Smile and shake hands. Then cement your social
success by sending a handwritten thank-you note within 24 hours
of the event.

Email and Social Media Savvy

Computers have facilitated an information explosion that makes the Age of Enlightenment look more and more like a faint glimmer in the Dark Ages. We can write, call, or look at each other virtually any time of the day or night. We can obtain answers to questions in a matter of seconds. Whether those answers and that information are accurate or credible is often a different matter.

We are fast becoming more identifiable as an online presence than as a living, breathing, feeling human being. We are constantly barraged by sensory stimuli of all kinds. No wonder we turn increasingly to disciplines like yoga.

This chapter endeavors to set forth some guidelines and principles to help us preserve some modicum of individuality—without exposing ourselves to embarrassing comments, photos, or videos that can permanently affect our lives and careers in adverse ways. Our technology is nothing short of miraculous. Unfortunately, we humans frequently abuse it, and that can harm our relationships.

Even in today's world of decreasing face-to-face contact, we need to maintain the basic principles of courtesy and kindness; we need to mind our manners while dealing indirectly with each other.

Email Is Eternal

The "e" in email should remind us of two important "e" words: editing and eternal. Email demands our editing attention, because email is eternal. Just about all email embarrassments derive from forgetting those two fundamental principles.

General Email Principles

Remember the cardinal rule of cyber etiquette: if you would not say it face-to-face, don't say it online. Remember, too, that because email is a public medium, there's no such thing as a private email. There are times when it's far more effective and practical either to pick up the phone or actually meet with the individual. Only you can judge.

When you send an email, make sure you send it only to the people who really need to read it; don't automatically hit the "Reply All" button. Make sure the subject line is clear, timely, and instructive. Employ good grammar and usage, as well as punctuation. Avoid sarcasm and make an effort to be kind.

As with all good writing, your message should be concise. Keep your sentences short. Don't repeat. Avoid rambling, and avoid interrupting yourself with asides or irrelevant remarks. If it's a long message, break it up with short paragraphs. Be as precise and specific as possible. For example, "Can you get back to me by Friday?" is better than "Get back to me in a timely fashion," which is vague and unlikely to elicit a quick response.

Avoid the temptation to write in lowercase only, which makes the message look trivial and also harder to read. Capitalize where appropriate, but don't write in all capitals for emphasis. That's the equivalent of shouting (although writing everything in low-ercase isn't the equivalent of whispering). Underlining and bold fonts have the same negative effect on the reader as all caps, so don't use them. Avoid unwarranted use of colored fonts.

Edit yourself. Reread your message at least once with a cold and critical eye. Look for typos and grammatical slips. Break up overly long sentences. No matter how sure you are, recheck the address and header information. If your system has a spell-checker, use it, no matter how good a speller you think you are. If you don't have access to this tool, go to spellcheck.net, or look in a dictionary. The time it takes to look up a word is time well spent. Misspellings and typos can change the meaning of your message.

Be careful about peppering your work-life prose with emphatic symbols such as exclamation points or dollar signs. That's kids' stuff. In general, stay away from emoticons, those cutesy little icons that are supposed to express emotion (for example, ☺). This is no better than writing "ha ha" to let people know you're joking.

On a more personal level, if your relationship with the other person is very comfortable, it's fine to use emoticons, especially if the reader already has used them with you. In any case, though, it's a bad idea to use an emoticon to take the sting out of a sarcas-tic salvo, a questionable comment, or a risky joke. Much better not to write these at all.

Acronyms can be baffling for some people, even those who text all the time. In business, it's a good idea to steer clear of them. However, it's a good idea to be familiar with the most commonly used acronyms, such as the following.

Acronym Definitions for Email

Acronym	Definition
AFC	Away from computer
BTW	By the way
FYI	For your information
IMO	In my opinion
IOW	In other words
NRN	No response necessary
PLS	Please
TIA	Thanks in advance
WRT	With respect to

Our emails say a lot about us to the people who receive them. An email that looks haphazard creates the same impression of us as though we showed up for an important meeting or date with torn clothes, bare feet, and dirty fingernails. Don't risk it. Even though email is a casual medium, it's not a license to be sloppy.

Business Email

Picture your message being printed and displayed on a bulletin board. Your message will look a lot better and will reflect more favorably on you if it's neat. If your system isn't formatted so that the lines are from 60 to 80 characters long, you should arrange for your copy to follow this generally accepted standard. Tabs and centered or justified text can be lost in transmission. For dates, use numbers instead of words. (The form is MM/DD/YY. For example, Christmas Day would appear 12/25/12.) Type your message single-spaced and leave a line between paragraphs.

The bottom line is that neatness and care are emblems of self-respect and also show respect for those reading your message.

Use the subject line. It's helpful to the person who receives your message and may even be helpful to you, the writer. Selecting the correct subject can help you focus on the meat of your message.

Keep the subject message as brief as possible. Think of it more as a title than a headline. Brevity is also a virtue when it comes to the message. If the message is unavoidably long, use the word "long" on the subject line to tip off the recipient.

Don't use your email signature as a sort of vanity license plate, employing jokes, diagrams, and bumper-sticker wisdom. It just won't work in a business context, and might be misinterpreted in other contexts. What strikes you as hilarious might strike someone else as simple-minded. Your signature should contain only your name and contact information. How you sign your name tells the other person how you want them to address you. It's an indicator of how you see the relationship. For example, an email with James Weber typed at the bottom suggests a more formal relationship than one signed Jim Weber.

If you want to forward an email message, check with the original author of the message first. It's not only impolite to circulate another's words without permission, but it might also be an infringement of copyright law, or a violation of privacy. This applies even if the message is trivial or contains good news, such as, "Jack's team won the tournament." Always get permission before forwarding.

If you get an email message that was not intended for you, instead of forwarding it to the right person, send it back to the sender and let her know about the mistake.

Never pass around another's email address without permission. When emailing someone for the first time, it's a good idea to say where you got the email address. If it's from a business card or a website, for example, say so.

In sending email internationally, it's a good idea to keep the language relatively formal. For one thing, citizens in many other countries are generally more formal in their business dealings, and it's customary for them to write even more formally than they speak.

Casual language can present difficulties in cross-cultural communications. Certain slang words or phrases have quite different meanings elsewhere, so watch what you write; also avoid clichés and jargon. Remember also that in many countries, age and rank are treated with a great deal more deference than in the United States.

BONUS POINTS

As David Shipley writes in his book *SEND*, "Please is a slippery word." In certain situations, it can convey an impatient, irritated tone. For example, "Would you please be sure to turn off the lights before you leave" makes the reader feel as though the author perceives her as lacking the common sense to turn out the lights. On the other hand, asking a person to "Please review the attached" would be appropriate. When in doubt, leave the "please" out. "Thank you" is less ambiguous, always welcome, and more easily understood when the favor already has been done. Thanking someone in advance can be obnoxious.

When people do you a small favor, it's entirely appropriate to thank them with an email. However, if they have gone out of their way to be gracious, helpful, or generous, such as taking you to dinner, giving you a gift, or helping you get a job, go out of your own way to put pen to paper after the first spontaneous email thank-you. Or, at the very least, follow up your email with a telephone call.

BONUS POINTS

When someone sends you an email thank-you, you don't have to respond. Sometimes an email sets off a chain of thank-you craziness. For example, I do you a favor. You email me a thank-you. I thank you for your considerate thank-you, and so it goes, on and on. Nip such nutsiness in the bud before it blooms.

Condolences by email can take advantage of the immediacy of the medium, especially when someone is part of the fabric of your daily life. They always are appreciated. However, follow up the email with a handwritten condolence letter because condolence letters are treasured, saved, and reread often.

When you apologize by email, make sure to write the word "Sorry" or "Apology" in the subject line, so that the other person doesn't ignore your message. The emailed apology is only the beginning of behavior that must include making amends. For example, "I'm so sorry that I lost your favorite key chain" is hollow unless you do your best to actually replace the item.

It's not a good idea to cc anyone on an apology without permission. Sometimes the other person would prefer to keep the matter quiet and forget about it. Copying others only serves to keep the whole incident alive.

It's best never to send emails when you're angry or upset. Those messages are destined to come back to haunt you, and they most often backfire.

Even the most vigilant of us mess up on email. You might have sent the wrong information to the wrong person, or made snarky comments and then sent them to the target of your criticism. The list of possible email faux pas is endless. This is not the time to try to make it right by sending another email. This is the time to get on the phone to sort it out, or to show up in person to clean up the mess. Nothing short of that will do.

Phones

Telephone communication, in one form or other, can be too easily taken for granted.

About 70 percent of the impression you make during a telephone conversation depends on vocal quality, so speak clearly and think about the tone of your voice. It's true—a smile can be "heard" over the telephone. Answer your ringing phone with either "Hello" or by identifying yourself right away, such as "Todd Jameson speaking" or "This is Sandy Chalmers" when it's a business line. Maintain a constant distance from the mouthpiece.

When you're on a call, don't engage in nonverbal communications with someone else in the room—smiling, grimacing, and so on. Don't engage anyone else in the room when on a call unless you let the person you're talking with know. For example, "Doug, just let me hand this package to the delivery service." Avoid speed-talking; if what you have to say is important enough to be said, make sure you say it slowly enough to be understood.

Limit your calling to between the hours of 9 A.M. and 9 P.M. unless you're sure the other person doesn't mind. Remember the differences in time zones, too. Don't chew gum or food. If you sneeze or cough, apologize. And never make phone calls from the bathroom stall, private as it might seem. In one way or another, the person you're calling will figure out where you are. Ending your calls on a positive note will make the other person feel upbeat, and so will you.

BONUS POINTS

When you call someone, identify yourself and ask if it's a good time to talk before you plunge into a conversation. Remember, unless we have a telephone call scheduled for that purpose, all telephone calls are interruptions.

Wrong numbers warrant an apology rather than a hang-up. Just say, "Sorry. I meant to call …." If you're answering someone else's phone, say "Janet Baker's line. This is Todd Jameson," so the caller doesn't think she got a wrong number.

Whether you're on a landline or a cell phone, be considerate when using the speaker function. Avoid beginning a conversation on the speaker. If you do, mention before the conversation begins that you're on a speaker phone. But preferably begin the conversation with your handset and ask if you can switch to speaker, explaining why: "We're all here at Dad's and want you to know we miss you." Identify every person in the room (or car, if you're not alone). Only one person should speak at a time, and that person should move closer to the phone. The person speaking should identify herself each time because the instrument distorts voices.

Avoid simultaneous conversations. If you have to leave during the call, say so. Never use a speakerphone for one-on-one conversations, because the other person will soon feel that you're dividing your attention. If you're put on speaker phone without being told, simply ask the person who called, "Am I on speaker?" Don't hesitate to ask to be taken off speaker, and if the caller balks, suggest a better time to talk.

Cell Phones and Smartphones

Telephone booths are a thing of the past. They were created with the idea that only the person you were calling should hear what you were saying. That's still a useful concept when using your cell phone. Be respectful and allow a distance of about 10 feet from others when on the phone.

Cell phones can bring us peace of mind if they help us do our job better. They also bring us joy when we want to congratulate someone spontaneously or tell someone far away that we love them. Yet in their glory lies their misfortune. A telephone call always will be an interruption, an intrusion. Cell phones make it possible to intrude into every single area of our lives, and that isn't a good and glorious thing.

Showing respect for others' time and space is something we should all practice. We need to keep in mind the telephone's power for disruption and be sensitive to that.

What does your ringtone say about you? It's one thing to be able to identify a ringing phone as yours. It's another thing to brand yourself with "Born to Be Wild" if that's not exactly the impression you want others to have of you.

If you're not expecting an urgent call, turn the cell phone off during business meetings, at social gatherings, in restaurants, in hospitals, in places of worship, and at the theater. If you must keep the cell phone on, rely on the vibrate mode. If you absolutely must keep your phone on during a meeting, explain in advance. If you must make a call at a social gathering or at a restaurant, excuse yourself and find a reasonably private place in which to make the call. If you must speak while others are near, speak softly. Your conversation might be fascinating to you, but it's intrusive for others. Don't ask to borrow someone's cell phone unless it's an emergency.

As a matter of your own safety, and the safety of others, don't talk and drive, and don't talk while crossing the street. Some states outlaw handheld cell phone use while driving, and statistics prove that the number of accidents drops with less cell phone usage. If you use your cell phone while driving, there may be dire consequences. If you need to make a call while driving, pull over, and take the few minutes you need to make your call. It's not worth risking your life—or that of others.

Be careful, very careful, when taking photos with your phone. Never take a photo of another person without permission or at least the full knowledge of the person you're photographing. If you wouldn't be so presumptuous with a regular camera, what makes you think you can take more liberties with your cell phone camera? You aren't a paparazzi!

Although asking permission before shooting the shot may take some of the "jokes" out of life, it's the one certain way not to offend. Sensitivity to the subjects of the pictures must come before the picture taker's sense of fun. The bottom line: photograph others as you would have them photograph you. If you wouldn't like some of your actions immortalized, don't immortalize those same actions of others.

BONUS POINTS

With Bluetooth technology you can appear very important, or simply crazy. You get to choose. Walking down the street, your earpiece covered by your hair, chatting incessantly, you might give the impression that you've lost your marbles. On the other hand, if your job or a situation requires you to constantly be on the phone, Bluetooth technology can be wonderful. Never keep your earpiece on when having a face-to-face conversation, or when you're at a party. Others will conclude that you don't consider them worth your full attention.

Texting

Texting is helpful because you can instantly get a message to another person without her phone having to ring. Still, indiscriminate texting is not a good idea. Not everybody has unlimited text message plans yet. Make sure you keep your messages shorter than three lines. Otherwise, send them as an email, or call the person and talk with them. Double-check your address book to be sure that you're sending the text to the right person, and if you're texting someone for the first time, identify yourself.

It's rude to text at theater performances, movies, concerts, or anywhere the light is intentionally dim. The backlight of the phone as you text is distracting and annoying. It's also rude, not to mention bad strategy, to text during meetings and meals. It's preferable to avoid texting bad news, or anything embarrassing or sensitive.

Don't expect an immediate reply to a text; not everybody is glued to their phones. And never mistakenly believe that texting is a substitute for meaningful dialogue or good grammar. Abbreviations and acronyms are fine when texting. Following are some of the most common.

Acronym Definitions for Texting

Acronym	Definition
AAMOF	As a matter of fact
AFAIK	As far as I know
BF	Boyfriend
BFF	Best friend forever
BRB	Be right back
BTW	By the way
CYE	Check your email
FWIW	For what it's worth
GF	Girlfriend
HTH	Hope this helps
IDK	I don't know
IMHO	In my humble opinion
LOL	Laughing out loud
LYLAS	Love you like a sister
NBD	No big deal
NFN	Not for nothing
TTYL	Talk to you later
YOLO	You only live once

Texting while driving is even more hazardous than talking on a cell phone, since you have to take your eyes off the road repeatedly. There can be no justification for cell phone use of any kind while driving. Pull over and send your message, and then turn the device off so you have no further temptation to use it until you get to a safe stopping point.

Voicemail

Although voicemail is being used less and less, it does remain part of life and business.

> **BONUS POINTS**
>
> Not everybody listens to voicemail messages. Many young people simply look at their missed call record on cell phones and dial auto return. The over-50 set is learning these new habits, yet still does rely on voicemail messages by both leaving them and listening to them. Keep this in mind when phone calling involves crossing generations. Keep in mind, too, that voicemail is still used in business, where landlines are more prevalent than cell phones as primary telephone numbers.

Your own answering greeting should be short. Don't bother to say that you aren't available to take the call. That's a waste of time and there's no point in restating the obvious. Instead, simply identify yourself and ask the caller to leave a message. If you really mean it, say you'll return the call as soon as possible. For example, "This is Mary Mitchell. Please leave a message, and I will call you back." If you want to give another option to reach you, go ahead, but limit it to only one telephone number or email address.

When you leave a voicemail message, be sure to identify yourself right away. Give your return phone number at the beginning of your message so that the other person doesn't have to listen to you twice. Speak slowly and clearly. It helps to pretend to be writing your number in the air, which will slow you down and help with clarity. Say when you can be reached.

If there are specific messages, be concise, and let the person know at the beginning so she can be listening for the information. For example, "I'm calling to let you know two things. First, I got the information about the game. Second, I will meet you in front of the box office at 6:30. See you then." Then just hang up. You don't need to say good-bye.

Don't use voicemail as a way to avoid speaking with someone. It doesn't help, and a person would have to be terminally dense not to figure out your game. If you must call when you know the other person isn't available, say, "I know you won't be able to take the call now, but I wanted to let you know that ...."

Phone calls deserve to be answered within a day. Even if it's not convenient to have a conversation, go ahead and return the call, indicating when you'll be available to talk. Sometimes sending an email to this effect works just as well as a quick phone call.

Social Networking

The primary thing to remember about social media is that it's forever. Once your posting is out there, it's out there. That means you really don't get second chances to present yourself well. Whether you use social media for personal or business use, your postings represent choices you make about how you want others to perceive you.

Familiarize yourself with the privacy settings so that you can control postings to your site. Unfortunately, even with strict privacy settings, nothing prevents someone with access to your postings from cutting and pasting the post and sharing it. (Ideally, they would ask your permission first, but the internet is the Wild West of modern technology, where often anything goes.) If you're new to a site, ask friends who might already be on the site to share their experiences with you. All social media sites are somewhat different; they have their own rules and guidelines. Each attracts its own audience.

In LinkedIn, for example, your professional headline is critical; make sure it's a one-sentence snapshot of your professional experience. Seek out recommendations from others regarding your character and work ethic; you can offer them a quid pro quo as an incentive. Customize your page to allow your personality to show. Consider a portfolio add-in. Join discussion groups, or start a new one. Make yourself available by posting your email and phone number, if you're comfortable doing so.

Social media has become a tool for prospective employers to screen job applicants, to the extent that social networking is essential for standing out in the job market today. That's a good argument for keeping your postings to something you would not mind your mother seeing. It's a good argument to forget about pictures of yourself in a drunken, half-clad stupor. It's also a good argument for being polite, using good grammar and punctuation, and editing, editing, editing whatever you post.

Rather than take all the fun and spontaneity out of posting on social media, well-chosen and edited postings add value to the time others invest to look at what you have to say. That means they'll return and be glad they did. Make your posts short, and people will be more likely to want to come back for more. Think of your posts as headlines, rather than articles. Set a mannerly tone, no matter how crass the comments to which you are responding may be. The high road is often lonely, yet worth taking.

Utilize social media add-ons for Microsoft Outlook, Gmail, or your web browser. These allow you to keep aware of others' social media updates, which will improve your ability to get acquainted or keep in touch.

Posting Pictures

Select a flattering yet informal profile picture. The idea here is to look accessible and engaging. Your photo also will help others determine if you're the right John Smith when they search. Make sure all your profile claims are accurate. If you didn't really win a Nobel prize, don't pretend that you did. It's all too easy to uncover the truth, and rebuilding lost trust is tough at best. Count to 10 before you let loose with a string of nasty comments and complaints. For one thing, tomorrow might find you with a change of heart and mind. For another, nastiness speaks well of nobody.

If you want to tag people in a photo, get their permission first. Make sure you select the Facebook setting to be notified whenever someone tags your photo—and then check often to make sure you're okay with posted photos. Never use the "poke" feature in a business context, and use it cautiously in a personal context because it can be misunderstood as sexual advances. When you come across posts that are questionable, snarky, or gossipy, don't pass them along. Let them die a natural death.

Friending and Unfriending on Facebook

You don't have to accept every request to be a contact or a friend. Simply ignore the request, even if it's repeated. When you want to add someone to your own list, think quality rather than quantity. It's a good policy to know the people you agree to friend. If there's someone you'd like to make a contact but you don't know, explain the reason you're making the request.

Unfriending someone is a simple matter and needs no apology if the relationship makes you uncomfortable in any way. Similarly, no explanations need be given when you untag a photo of yourself.

Tweeting

Tweeting is all about giving information in real time. In your brief Twitter profile, start with an intriguing bio, plus a URL to your personal or work sites, depending upon your purpose. Making sure that information you tweet is constructive is the challenge. Nobody wants to know what you had for breakfast. But if you read a useful, illuminating article while you were having breakfast, it makes sense to tweet the link to the article. Twitter followers are interested in similar topics, and they follow individuals who have something to offer their knowledge base.

Ask yourself what value you can add to others' experience, and be gracious about retweeting others' posts, especially when they can encourage discussion. Thank others who retweet your posts. Decide whether you want to link your tweets to your Facebook or LinkedIn pages. Remember that your friends might not be amused with a multitude of daily postings, so it might be better to keep some accounts separate. Here again, make sure your posts could be rated PG. Never share confidential information. The internet is forever.

Blogging and Commentary

Blogging gives us an opportunity to share our experiences, expertise, and opinions in community spaces. Blogging has changed journalism forever because it offers an open dialogue without filters. That is the good news, and also the bad news.

Participating on someone else's blog isn't an invitation to be abrasive, rude, nasty, or insensitive. When someone takes the time to thoughtfully write on a subject, it's pretty disrespectful to comment "What a jerk you are!" simply because you happen to disagree. Make sure your comments support a point of view rather than share a series of expletives that help no one. You don't have to be mean to be tough with your views, and it's a useful exercise to learn to say provocative things civilly.

Most blogs have their own rules, so make sure you learn them before you participate. Don't spam blogs. Bloggers generally have to approve content to the blog, and it's a huge imposition to expect anyone to waste precious time to trash useless comments. Remember that when you blog, you're joining a group of people you don't know. Look before you leap. Get a sense of the blog's direction and followers. Make sure you pay attention to the code of conduct. Never post any false information. Most of all, remember that once you've posted it, there's no turning back.

The Write Way

In these days of electronic mail, you might never have purchased a postage stamp. Yet it's probably a safe bet that when and if you've received an envelope with your name written by hand, and a note or an invitation inside, you felt pretty special. It's also a pretty safe bet that, feeling special yourself, you felt that the person who wrote to you was special, too.

Whether you write to say thank you, send congratulations, express condolence, extend an invitation, or apologize, your small investment of time and resources will garner you a tremendous return. Your effort to connect will set you apart from the people who don't bother to express themselves in the first place, as well as those who choose to connect through technology. When we've gone out of our way to help someone; when we're grieving; when we've been wronged; when we have reason to celebrate—the pen is much mightier than the computer chip. A handwritten letter is so much more than an instrument for conveying facts.

In work life, a letter's very appearance makes a statement about your organization. The letter's style and content also speak clearly to your qualities as a person and as a professional.

In your personal life, a letter can be a gift that pleases both the sender and the receiver. It's more personal than a telephone call and often more intimate and touching than a private conversation. To the recipient, a handwritten note on fine paper is so much more meaningful than an email. The letter can become part of a family's history or a valued keepsake.

Personal expression on paper has rarely enjoyed more breadth. Gone are the days when stationery was stodgy. Today people are building their stationery "wardrobes" in colors and styles that never have been more vibrant. At the same time, even a letter scrawled on a lined legal pad will be treasured when its message is sincere, authentic, and timely.

Maybe you could use an attitude adjustment about handwritten correspondence. Instead of thinking (or worse, saying in front of your kids), "I have to write so-and-so a thank-you note," replace the negative with the positive: "I get to write so-and-so a thank-you note today." Doing so will make you feel good, and receiving your note probably will make the recipient's day.

Thank-You Notes

Thank-you notes probably rank first in the hierarchy of written correspondence. They should be lively rather than the robotic, "Thank you for the present. It was nice of you to think of me." Not only is that boring to read, it's boring to write.

Every thank-you note should include these three components: Specific mention of whatever you're thanking the person for. (A gift? Taking you to lunch? Sending you some important information? Introducing you to someone you had wanted to meet?) Next, acknowledge the effort that went into making the gift possible. Finally, tell the person how you'll use the gift or how the gift benefited you. In its simplest form, such a letter might sound like, "Dear Aunt Polly, thank you so much for the electric blue sweater. You must have shopped all day to find my very favorite shade of blue. I can't wait to wear it to tomorrow's basketball game. Love, Julia."

Remember that our only true gifts are our time and our attention. Sometimes that translates into a physical object. Other times it translates into doing something for another—and those efforts deserve to be recognized. That is why the second sentence of a thank-you note should begin with "you" rather than "I." For example, "You're so busy that taking the time to connect me with your colleagues is very special, and I want to tell you how much I appreciate your help on my behalf." Or, "With all you have on your plate, you can't imagine how much pleasure your making time to find the perfect scarf brings me."

BONUS POINTS

What if the gift is awful, like the classic terrible crocheted sweater in a ghastly color that you'd rather not be seen in? Here's where you embrace the saying "It's the thought that counts." Look for the positive so that you can make an authentic comment. For example, you could say, "You were so kind to make me the beneficiary of your first crocheting project; the sweater is a treasure, and I treasure all the hours you spent making it for me."

The last sentence of the thank-you note tells the other person either how you'll use the gift, or what his efforts on your behalf mean to you. For example, "Because of all the insights you shared, I have a much better idea about how to stand out at my interview next week."

If you're thanking someone for a gift of money or a gift card, you don't have to specify the amount of the gift. All you need to do is reference his "generous gift." Of course, if there are other details that would make the giver feel even more appreciated, by all means include them. For instance, when someone makes something especially for you, or gives you a one-of-a-kind item, be sure to mention that thoughtfulness.

When you've been a houseguest, be sure to include little tidbits of what made the visit special. "Seeing paintings at the museum with you, an artist yourself, made the visit that much more memorable."

BONUS POINTS

Send a thank-you note whenever somebody sends you flowers or gives you a present; invites you to lunch or dinner; asks you to be a houseguest; or extends an invitation to a play, concert, or sports event. Don't forget to send one to anyone who does you a favor, provides some valuable information, or gives you a reference. These notes achieve more significance when they are sent out promptly.

Condolence Letters

Never let your own discomfort about death stop you from consoling the bereaved. A letter of condolence gets read and reread far more than any email or text message. Here's one instance where it almost doesn't matter what you say. What matters is that you say something. The wrong thing to say is nothing.

When someone is part of the everyday fabric of your life, an email takes advantage of the immediacy of the medium. There's nothing wrong with sending an email. However, handwritten letters become part of a person's family history. Letters are permanent; they are always there to share with our children when they're old enough to read and understand. It's a way of extending the memory of someone we loved.

Begin your letter by saying how sad the news is, and that you know the family must be suffering from the loss.

Recall some fond memories of the person who died in your letter. For instance, "I still can hear Jack cheering the Little League team to victory." Whatever kind, amusing recollections you might have that will bring a smile to the reader, include them. Don't be afraid of fun; perhaps there are practical jokes you played on each other. The more specific and personal you can be, the more the reader will appreciate what you say.

Say what kind of an impact the departed person had on your life, and what lessons you might have learned from him. Praise the individual for his accomplishments and character, such as "I'll never forget his good humor, his patience, and his kindness to all of us. He showed me how to hold my tongue when I felt angry and count to 10 before I spoke my mind. He always had my back, and it will be almost impossible to imagine our neighborhood without him." Offer to be of assistance in any possible way. Reassure the reader that you're keeping the entire family in your thoughts and heart.

You might not know the person who is deceased. Still, it's a very kind gesture to write a condolence letter to the bereaved member of the family whom you do know. That note might read like, "Although I never had the pleasure of meeting your mother, she must have been a remarkable woman to have such a wonderful daughter. I've heard others tell of what an important influence she has had on your life, your career, and your family. I'm very sorry for your loss, and I hope you'll find the strength and comfort you need to get you through this sad time."

Be careful to avoid emphasizing how much you feel bereaved personally. The object of a condolence letter is to comfort the person who has lost a loved one, not to make him feel sorry for you.

Letters of Apology

When you've hurt someone's feelings or caused a person undue trouble, spring into action. First, do your best to apologize in person. Follow that up with a letter of apology. It's important to state very clearly the effect your behavior or thoughtlessness had on someone. It's also important to offer to make amends if at all possible.

We are very quick to expect a prompt apology when someone wrongs us. By turns, then, we need to be willing to apologize quickly ourselves. It's never comfortable to apologize, yet when we let time pass before we do—or worse, we don't bother to apologize at all—we breed resentment in the person we have wronged. Big mistake all around.

For example, "Dear Marilyn, last night's snafu never should have happened, but it did. I can't tell you how embarrassed and sorry I am for missing your dinner party. I put it on the calendar for next week, which was careless and inconsiderate of me. Your dinner parties always are so extraordinary that frankly, I can't believe I actually blanked out on the date. You always lavish so much attention on not only serving delicious food, but also on every beautiful detail. You deserve much better attention from me, and I hope you'll forgive me for the worry and trouble I've caused. I also hope that you'll let me take you to dinner soon. I'll call you in the next couple of days."

Or, "I thought I was being so witty and clever when I made those remarks yesterday. In reality, I was being childish, inconsiderate, and probably seemed even arrogant. Please know that I never deliberately would hurt your feelings in a million years. I have no idea what came over me or how I could have been so clueless. I do know this: I've learned a lesson, and you can be sure that I'll be a lot less enthusiastic with my biting commentary in the future. I just hope you'll forgive me and we can put my stupid behavior behind us. You're an important friend to me, and I'll do better to be a worthy steward of that gift."

BONUS POINTS

Sending flowers really helps to soothe hard feelings when you've done something foolish. Try to match the flowers with the person's décor and taste as best you can. Consider the gift an investment in your relationship, pricey though it may be.

Letters of Congratulations

Letters of congratulations are the happiest ones to write, and they make an enormous difference to the people who receive them. Here again, the handwritten letter goes far beyond the electronic version to bring a smile to its reader.

Don't hold back on a letter even when the person you know isn't the one who actually won the award or achieved the distinction. Family members and close friends all feel part of the good news, and they appreciate being remembered.

Letters don't have to be long or formal. You can say something like, "Dear Maddy, congratulations on the study grant to go to Ghana. There's no doubt in my mind that you'll bring your students a wealth of solid information, coupled with compassion, kindness, and humor. That genuine, dazzling smile of yours will go a long way to making the world a better place. You'll learn as much from Ghana as Ghana learns from you, and I look forward to hearing the stories when you return. You go, girl!"

Or, "I heard the great news about John's promotion. You all must be so thrilled and proud. Congratulations!"

A Few Points for Any Letter

When you open a letter, the most formal salutation is "Dear So-and-So." If you know the person you're writing to, and are on a first-name basis, then use the first name. Otherwise, use "Mr." or "Ms." Be sure to use the correct honorific when you address the envelope. And don't forget to write your return address on the front-left corner of the envelope so that the post office can identify it quickly in case it needs to be returned for some reason.

MISERABLE MOMENTS

You hear that your best friend from high school has just lost his mother; she was like a second mother to you. Even though you had a falling out some years ago, you send a beautiful condolence letter. Yet you don't hear back. You assume that your former friend is still mad at you. Years later, you bump into him, and you can't help but ask why he never replied to your letter. He asks, "What letter?" Turns out he never received it. You used the old address, there was no forwarding address, and you forgot to put your return address on the envelope!

The way you close a letter should reflect the nature of your relationship with the recipient. A flat "Yours truly" will disappoint and might even offend a close friend. Leave the L-word alone unless the recipient is a very close friend. Some suggestions are "Fondly," "Affectionately," "Warmly," "Best regards," "Regards"—or simply sign your name.

When you're really stumped for something to express how you feel, you might use a quote. For example, "No wise man ever wished to be younger" (Jonathan Swift) is always an appropriate birthday letter starter. Two good sources of quotations are *The Oxford Dictionary of Quotations* and *Bartlett's Familiar Quotations*.

How to Say It in Person

>>> **In This Chapter**

- Why small talk is a big skill
- Calming down heated situations so everyone is heard
- How to stop gossip
- Understanding taboos of talk
- Handling invitations and requests—and saying no

Whenever you talk face-to-face with another person, what she hears is more important than what you think you said. A bore is someone who thinks herself fascinating. A brilliant conversationalist is someone who makes you feel fascinating. It's all about tuning into the other person, even when you're stumped about what to say and how to say it.

Small Talk

There's nothing small about small talk. It is, in fact, a very big skill and immeasurably important. It goes a long way to put the other person at ease, and it gives you a pretty good idea whether that relationship is going anywhere.

Conversation Triggers

If you want to be interesting to your conversation partners, be interested in them. Listen, really listen, to what they have to say. Don't drift off thinking about what you'll say next when there's a lull in the dialogue. Everybody has a story, and most of us think ours is pretty interesting. Getting the ball rolling often is the biggest challenge. But it doesn't have to be.

For example, you might ask an easy-to-answer question about your surroundings. That might sound like, "On the way here I noticed that there are four coffee shops on one intersection. Do you ever wonder how they all stay in business?" That might lead to a discussion of who prefers which one, what the area industries are that feed it, and whether the other person is used to seeing so much coffee competition.

Asking open-ended questions is a pivotal tactic. You might say, "What do you like to do when you aren't working? What do you do for fun?" Other such questions might include "How would you compare our city to other places where you've lived?", "What made you decide to get into this kind of work?", or "What did you like best about your vacation?"

It's helpful to introduce yourself in terms of what you do rather than your title. That gives the other person a bridge to engage you in conversation. When I say, "I'm Mary Mitchell. I write a column about manners for kids," the responder is always more genuinely interested than when I say I am president of a consulting firm.

It's also nice to tell the other person something helpful or something you think she might find interesting. For instance, "I heard you say you enjoy biking. Did you know that there are no fewer than half a dozen cycling clubs in the area? I'm glad to give you some information about them."

Even a subject as seemingly banal as the weather can be a good conversation tool. For example, "Isn't today glorious? It's so good to see the sun after so much rain." Or you might ask, "Are you from this area?" The answer might be yes, and then you can ask the other person what she likes best about living there. If the answer is something like, "No, I'm from Ohio," then you can ask her what it was like growing up in the Midwest, and what brought her to your town. Whatever you discuss, remember to keep the subject upbeat.

It's surprising how true confessions connect us. Nothing encourages people to start talking like a desire to get others to start talking. Try this: "I don't know anybody here. I find big parties like this kind of overwhelming. How do you know the host?"

If you want to become a certified good conversationalist, you'll need to master the following:

- Limit "I" in your conversations and focus on "you."
- Speak clearly and simply, using good grammar and clean language.
- Don't boast about yourself and your possessions or accomplishments.
- Let others change the topics they might have started.
- Remain upbeat and positive and make direct eye contact, avoiding depressing topics and malicious gossip.

It's always useful to cultivate a good sense of humor without attempting to be a comedian. Any jokes you tell ought to be appropriate and audible to your group. Welcome others into the group. Try to bring out the best in everyone. Be sure to respect others' privacy and professionalism; for example, don't ask whether a person in the group is happy with her face-lift.

Learn to discuss topics that don't necessarily interest you. Don't pretend to know foreign languages or make important statements unless you're sure of the facts.

Before you go to any event, ask yourself the following four questions: *Who am I?* Are you a job applicant, on a first date, at a PTO meeting? *Where am I?* Do you know something about the city you're in? Is the format of the occasion formal or casual? *To whom am I speaking?* What do you know about your hosts? Have you ever met this person before? *How do I want them to perceive and respond to me?* Are you looking to be hired, or for a date? Is this a club you want to join? Being able to engage others, put them at ease, and bring out the best in them is the essence of good manners.

Body Language

Body language is important. Even if you're speaking the right words, your body might be contradicting them. Be sure to stand upright, but not at attention. Don't shift your weight around as if you're preparing to return a tennis serve. Don't fold your arms. It's distracting. Keep your hands away from your face. Don't slap others on the back, take their arms, or engage in physical contact. Don't watch other people moving about the room while someone is talking to you.

Giving and Receiving Compliments

Giving compliments can be easy enough; sometimes receiving them is difficult for people. When you give a compliment, make it genuine and follow it up with a question: "These cookies you made are delicious. Have you always been interested in baking?" or, "I learned a lot about planting from your description of how those fuchsias grow. When did you get into gardening, or were you just born with a green thumb?" And be specific. For example, "The examples you gave about the building's safety code really helped me to not resent all the rent we're paying."

Everybody likes to be acknowledged and appreciated. Use the person's name if you know it, but be careful not to overuse it.

There's no reason ever to give an insincere compliment. Few things are as transparent as a phony or forced compliment, and few things can wreck your credibility faster. If you don't mean it, don't say it.

When you're on the receiving end of the compliment, don't qualify or diminish it. That just tells the person who complimented you that her judgment is off. Instead, smile, say "thank you," and leave it at that. Or you might say something like, "I'm glad you thought so" or, "I'm glad you like it."

 MISERABLE MOMENTS

You are feeling trapped in a small group, where the conversation has gone from boring to stultifying. Breaking away from a conversation can be just as difficult as getting one started. Yet every conversation runs its course. If yours has, make sure to acknowledge the other person with something like, "Glad we could catch up." Then, "I need to say hello to [so-and-so] before I leave." It's honest. It's kind. It's acceptable. Excuses such as, "I'm going to refill my drink" can backfire if you have a full glass, and "The food looks delicious. I think I'll have some," can open the door for the other person to join you.

Calming Communications

To help defuse resentment and hostility in heated situations, use "I" language. Substituting "I" for "you" can help you avoid a defensive response. For example, imagine someone saying to you, "Do you understand? Are you sure?" Now, imagine the same person saying, "I've been over this so often that I might not be coming across clearly. Please let me know if I've skipped any questions you might have had."

Avoid zingers and sarcasm, too. The word *sarcasm* comes from the Greek word *sarcous*, meaning "to rip and tear the flesh." If that is not your intention, don't be sarcastic. For example, "Your hair looks nice today; you must have washed it." When we zing somebody, that person's natural reaction is to zing back. Soon, we're more interested in zinging than listening or communicating.

Avoid chasing rabbits—don't go off on another topic or stray from the agenda. Studies tell us that our first reaction to straying off topic is confusion, followed by impatience and resentment. Not sticking to the point creates a negative emotional reaction in others.

Also, don't interrupt. It's not only rude, but it also creates the opposite of what we want when we interrupt. Interruptions lengthen conversations rather than shorten them because the person being interrupted initially thinks, *They didn't hear me*, and begins over, or *They didn't understand*, and backtracks. After being interrupted a couple of times, the speaker feels frustrated and resentful, like being pushed back down a mountain after having struggled to reach the top.

Always be sure to listen. When someone believes you're not listening, her reaction is to feel demeaned, disrespected, and unimportant. Take mental notes. That will keep you focused, and the other person will know that you're engaged.

Restate what you heard. For example, "If I've understood you correctly, you feel that the problem can be solved by negotiating, rather than by going to court. Is that correct?" Ask questions that clarify and avoid beginning questions with "why." That tends to create a defensive reaction. Instead, use "who," "what," "when," "where," and "how." Stay in the present tense. References to the past too often connote blame and generate defensive responses.

Don't disparage feelings. Don't tell someone how to think or feel—that's a judgment. Saying "That's a silly way to feel about this" or "I can't believe you feel that way" causes defensiveness.

Don't use absolutes. For example, "You're always late" only makes the other person try to come up with the one time she was on time. Rather, talk about behaviors you've seen or would like to see. Try, "I noticed that you were nearly an hour late for work on Tuesday, Thursday, and Friday. Our work day begins at 8, so please make sure you're ready to begin then."

Remember to calm yourself down before you blast anyone about her behavior or before you offer criticisms of anyone's performance to a third party. Again, stick to observable facts. For example, "I'd appreciate if you could make certain that your cashiers pay attention to the order of customers in line. I waited for 10 minutes, only to have someone cut in front with a question that took another 5 minutes to answer."

Stop the Gossip

Gossip wastes time and, when it's malicious, hurts people. Mindless gossip is just silly and makes the tale-teller look far worse than the target. When someone comes to you with what she thinks is juicy gossip, don't take the bait. Instead, take the (often lonely) high road. Change the topic of conversation. That might sound like, "Life is too short to get entangled in this stuff. Besides, I'd like to know what you think of ...."

Or simply drift away. You don't need to say a word. Just remove yourself from the scene, or the group of gossips. Your silence and absence will be eloquent. If you prefer to stay put, rise to the defense. Say things like, "That just doesn't sound like John," or, "That really is not the way I heard it." Then, "It's really not fair to belabor this when John can't be here to defend himself." Avoid sweeping statements such as, "You're unfair." Remember that the moment we begin a sentence with "you," communication stops while the other person builds a defense.

Speak the truth to the right person when you learn that a rumor is untrue. Take the person who's spreading it around aside and straighten the score. That might sound like, "I thought you'd be interested to know that, as a matter of fact, John really did graduate with honors from college. I was in his class." Period. No lecturing; just the facts, spoken in as unemotional and flat a tone as though you were saying, "It's raining outside."

Deflect, don't report, since no good can come of repeating petty rumors to those being rumored about. It just hurts, and there's the clear and present danger that the messenger will be "shot." When you hear a serious untruth being spread about someone, immediately and passionately rise to the defense. That might sound like, "I don't believe that information for a single moment. If it does happen to be true, there must have been a very good reason for it that we don't know. What I do know is that I'm not willing to stand here and be a party to a story that maligns a good person. Get somebody else to listen." Don't raise your voice! In fact, the slower and lower you speak this, the more you'll command the other person's attention.

MISERABLE MOMENTS

The more you badmouth someone else, the more harm you do yourself, without even realizing it. Most people love to listen to gossip, so they won't object to your rambling on about somebody else's foibles. But ultimately, in their minds, they'll think of you unkindly and worry about what you might be saying about them.

Talk Taboos

Sometimes we're nosy. Sometimes we're impulsive. Sometimes we genuinely want to know. Nevertheless, don't ask people, especially those who appear to be over the age of 30, their age. And don't try to be slick and try to figure it out by asking what year they graduated from high school or college.

You don't need to know how much people weigh. You certainly have no right to inquire about a past prison experience. How much money they have or issues relating to confidential business matters are not your concern. You may be curious, but you really don't need to know why they left the company, about the price of their home, about the size of their mortgage or what they pay in rent, or what kind of deal they got on anything.

And there are other topics to keep away from—for instance, serious health matters, such as how chemotherapy or psychotherapy are progressing—unless the other person brings the subject up.

You might open a can of worms by inquiring why a spouse or significant other is not at the party, about their sex life, the status of their marriage, terms of their divorce, or why they're not drinking. You're asking for trouble if you broach the subjects of political leanings, same-sex marriage, abortion, or immigration rights.

Handling Invitations and Requests Face-to-Face

If you're doing the inviting, above all, be specific. That should sound like, "Can you come to our house Sunday at 5 for pizza? We'll be watching the big game." Be sure not to corner the person you're inviting in such a way as to make her feel obliged to attend your function.

BONUS POINTS

What if someone asks you to be the recording secretary for the PTO meeting and you would prefer to have a root canal than take the job? Simply depersonalize the situation. Saying "That won't work for me" goes down a lot easier than "I can't do that." Tell the other person what you can do instead of what you can't do. "I'm glad to bring healthy snacks for the meeting. I'm sure you can find somebody else to keep minutes." Smile. Don't roll your eyes or heave a sigh.

If you've been invited but the answer is "no" for whatever reason, be sure to say something like, "Sorry, but I have other plans that afternoon. Thanks so much for thinking of me, though." You don't need to explain. You could be planning to watch your plants grow or the paint dry.

Either way—yes or no—be sure to RSVP within 24 hours. Don't wait until the last moment in hopes that something better will come along.

On the Go

Ah, to travel. To get out of your routine and see new places, visit old friends, and see faraway family members. Vacation. Business trips. Reunions. Picnics.

Your experiences will be memorable, that's for certain. But will they be good? Or will the trip be a nightmare? Certain things that affect the outcome one way or the other will be beyond your control. Yet with proper behavior and appropriate responses, you can make the best of a tough situation, thereby salvaging the trip.

Cars

In recent years, road rage has become all too common. Whether this phenomenon occurs because transportation by automobile has become impossibly frustrating, or because we're always in such a hurry to get wherever we're going, or because we have so little control over the rest of our lives, the fact is that our roadways at times become combat zones.

Flipping each other off, intentionally slowing down on the highway, or tailgating to antagonize the other guy are becoming commonplace. Choose not to respond to provocations or escalations; after all, cars are large machines traveling at a fast pace, and therefore dangerous.

The Courteous Driver

If you fall into this category, you wear your seat belt, keep your eyes on the road, and drive defensively. You don't apply makeup while the car is moving, nor do you text, read the paper, or talk on your cell phone. You don't turn the radio up to blaring levels or listen to your iPod through ear buds, because you know you need to be able to hear another car's horn. You signal before turning. And you don't pound your horn the split second the light turns green because the driver in front of you has less-than-split-second reactions.

If the driver behind you is tailgating, or, worse, flashing lights or honking, move over and let him pass. There's no point in obstinately staying in the passing lane, even if you're driving as fast as you think cars in this stretch of the road should be going. Who knows what could happen if the person behind you were to lose it completely? Stay cool and let the aggressor zoom past. The police will catch up to him sooner or later.

The Courteous Passenger

If you're a courteous passenger, you don't distract the driver, nor ask the driver to take unnecessary risks. You offer to get the money out for the tollbooths, and to pay for gas when appropriate. You're a second set of eyes looking out for road hazards. If licensed, you offer to help with the driving. Or you ask, "Would you like me to navigate?" This is better than barking uninvited directional commands.

Whether you're the driver or passenger, don't even think about eating smelly food in the car or smoking, even with the windows down.

Taxis

Make sure the meter starts at the accepted baseline; if there's no meter, be sure you're clear on what the fare will be for your ride. If you're certain that you're being overcharged, settle the issue before you let the driver get going.

BONUS POINTS

Be courteous in hailing a cab. If you see an elderly person trying for the same cab, let him have it. There will be plenty more where that one came from.

As a passenger, you have the right to ask your driver not to talk on his cell phone while driving, to observe the speed limits, and to not drive as though he were rushing his wife in labor to the hospital. Give clear directions, if you know how to get where you're going, and object if you see that the driver is headed in exactly the wrong direction. Phrase it like this: "Excuse me, but I am sure that we should be heading in the opposite direction; I have been here before."

Trains and Buses

Using these modes of transportation, especially trains, can be a memorable, charming experience. The charm fades fast, however, if the person next to you is crowding your seat, eating smelly food, talking loudly on his cell phone, wearing powerful scents, or smelling like he hasn't bathed in a month. You don't have to sit and suffer; you can always get up and find another place. No explanation is needed; simply excuse yourself and move.

Many trains now have "quiet cars," where travelers are expected to shut off their cell phones. If a fellow passenger violates the rules, ask the conductor to handle it. Should you be able to catch the offender's eye, you might pleasantly put your finger to your lips as a reminder.

If you can grab an Amtrack Red Cap, he will take you and your luggage onto the quiet car before general boarding, assuring you of a seat. This is worth the cost of the tip, which you should give to the porter—around $2 a bag.

Subways and light rails can get extremely overcrowded during rush hour. Be as considerate as you can be: let exiting passengers out; don't block the doors, so that passengers may enter; and if you see someone who is elderly or who is carrying a heavy burden, stand up and offer your seat. Use ear buds for your music players, and don't play the music so loud that everyone in the car can hear it.

BONUS POINTS

Have your bus fare ready so you don't hold up other passengers trying to get on.

Buses, except for the double-decker varieties, offer the advantage of having the driver share the same compartment with the passengers. Offensive behavior will often attract the driver's attention, and meaningful intervention may then be expected. Failing this, and if you aren't comfortable confronting the offender, walk up the aisle and present your complaint to the person behind the wheel. Be careful how you speak to the driver. Leave out sarcasm, swearing, and expletives. Restrain yourself from judging and simply state observable fact and behavior.

Airplanes

There was a time when flying was an enjoyable experience. Not anymore—not since 9/11—nor is it likely to be ever again. Virtually all flights are full and often overbooked, and airports are almost always crowded.

Getting to the Gate

Delays at security gates are the norm. Keep a cool head; practice yogic breathing (slow breaths, pushing the belly forward during the inhalation, and pulling it in while you exhale). Anticipate that the person in front of you will be frustratingly slow, while the person behind you practically will be breathing down your neck. There's no reason not to give the TSA workers a pleasant smile; it won't get you through the line any faster, but it might help make the experience less stressful.

Boarding

While boarding, practice consideration and kindness. Give the flight attendants a smile and a sincere greeting. Be careful not to wipe out any knees or shoulders as you lug your carry-ons down the aisle. Mind that you don't swing your backpack around, knocking against the heads of seated passengers. Be prepared with all of your medications, neck rests, blankets, and books, so that you can stash your carry-on quickly and get into your seat.

Remember that the most important things you can carry on are your smile and your polite demeanor. And you won't want to stow these overhead until the trip is over; keep them with you and ready to access at all times.

Say hello to the passenger sitting next to you. You aren't obliged to entertain him throughout the flight, but an effort to acknowledge one another will make later cooperation more likely. After all, you may need to get up and use the facilities or stretch. Be polite about this. Who knows, you may end up making a new friend or a useful business contact!

No matter where you sit, don't hog the armrests. The typical three-seat row has four armrests, and you may have commandeered two for yourself, but recognize that there is no such thing as squatter's rights, especially on a long flight. Let your seatmate have his chance once in a while.

Obese passengers have to make a special effort not to overcrowd their neighbors. If you're next to a plus-sized passenger, recognize that they are aware of their girth and avoid sighs and eye rolling as you slide into your seat.

If there are children flying with you, you have a particular responsibility to see that they don't disturb the other passengers. If you're fortunate enough to have a fellow passenger in your row who exhibits friendly behavior toward your child, don't immediately surrender the baby-sitting duties and go to sleep. Your child is your responsibility.

Children flying unaccompanied sometimes present real problems. Flight attendants don't have time to mind your child, and the person sitting next to him wasn't anticipating taking on extra duties either. Pack your child off with enough diversions to keep him occupied throughout the flight. If he is hyperactive or unruly, you'll need to send an adult along with him.

If you're ill, it's unfair to expose other passengers to your germs. With a medical excuse, you may be able to postpone your flight and not suffer serious financial penalties.

Remember that it's a good idea to look well groomed and well dressed when you travel, especially on planes. For one thing, you never know who you'll meet. For another, flight staffs will treat you better, especially when you run into unforeseen glitches such as delays and cancellations. As a courtesy to other passengers, avoid wearing powerful fragrances when you travel.

Bathrooms on planes get plenty of use. Be sure that when you get to the front of the line, you don't overstay your welcome; there are others waiting to use the facilities, too. Don't spend time perfecting your makeup; don't shave; don't balance your checkbook. Go in, do your business, clean up the sink and counter after yourself, and leave.

Being a Good Houseguest

Remember the adage from Ben Franklin that "Fish and house-guests smell after three days" and don't overstay your welcome. Make it clear from the outset that you'll be visiting for a finite period of time. Your hosts may ask you to stay on, but don't take them up on their offer. Always give them not quite enough of your presence, and they'll ask you back later for more. At the same time, realize that your presence may liven things up and be a welcome relief. Kahlil Gibran wrote, "If it were not for guests, all houses would be graves." So in these two quotes we see both sides of the coin.

As a guest, you're giving the gift of your time and attention to your hosts, who in turn are doing the same for you. These are the most precious gifts we have to give. Still, you should also bring along some other token. It need not be expensive; a good gift is one that displays some thoughtfulness on the part of the giver.

If you haven't a clue what to bring, after a short stay and a look around, you'll come up with something appropriate. Something typical of your part of the world when you're visiting a faraway place always seems to work. Taking your hosts out for dinner before you leave is appropriate. A gift certificate to Starbucks would be a bit too impersonal.

If your host doesn't spell out the agenda, ask what the scheduled plans are. Otherwise you might not bring the right clothes. Give your host some downtime, too. Say, "I'd like to go explore the farmers' market and local bake shops one morning. I know you've been there loads of times, and I'm glad to do this on my own." A host might say, "You'll be on your own most mornings while I clear the decks for the afternoon and evening to spend together."

Leave your guest room even neater than you found it. Be sure to send off a handwritten thank-you note to your hosts, preferably within a day of your departure, especially if you hope to be invited back again soon.

At the Hotel

Whether you're staying at a five-star resort, a Motel Six, or a bed and breakfast, you'll want to act as if you were a houseguest. Say "please" and "thank you." Dazzle the staff with your smile. Wish them a good day as you conclude your business. Preface requests with phrases like "if it isn't too much trouble." A little politeness will get you service that's more prompt and courteous.

You have a right to ask for a different room if what you've been shown isn't to your liking or isn't what you asked for when you made the reservation, or lacks a functioning heater, air conditioner, sink, toilet, or television. If your neighbors are too noisy, don't bang on walls or knock on doors, taking matters into your own hands. Ask hotel management to take care of the problem for you.

Unless you're staying at a club that specifies that the staff is not to be tipped, keep plenty of dollar bills on hand and disperse them liberally. Consider the doorman, if he does anything more than simply opening the door for you. Be sure to tip the porter who takes your bags in and anyone who brings them up to your room and shows you the location of all the conveniences; a dollar or two a bag is the norm. The maid deserves a few dollars each day. Housekeeping staff changes daily, so don't wait until you're checking out to leave a tip. Place the cash on the bed or on the bathroom counter so the housekeeper knows it's a daily tip. The waiter who brings up the tray if you order room service deserves a few dollars beyond the room service charge, which usually includes gratuity. The valet who parks and brings back your car when you're ready to leave should be tipped a couple of dollars, as should the doorman who hails you a taxi.

MISERABLE MOMENTS

Suppose that the hotel you've just checked into bears little resemblance to the secure and cozy nook you saw presented on the internet. You've already reserved a room with your credit card. You feel unsafe. You have a problem here.

If the place is really creepy, you simply must leave and deal with trying to get your money back later by phone, internet, or through the local Better Business Bureau.

Don't trash your hotel room just because a maid will tidy up after you. Hang your PJs up and stash your dirty laundry in a drawer or on a shelf, or, better yet, in your bag.

Out and About

Going out. A chance to put some pizzazz in the old routine. Shedding the T-shirts and blue jeans for a coat and tie, or a skirt with heels. Maybe just getting off the couch and fulfilling the New Year's resolution by joining a gym, and actually using your membership. Perhaps you're meeting an old friend for luncheon and a trip to the museum.

Wherever you're going, you'll be interacting with strangers. There are simple, minimal rules of conduct you'll want to observe. You may not be well versed in the finer points of etiquette, but you should know the importance of consideration and kindness. If you can keep these attributes in mind, you won't go wrong. You might step on a toe or two, but your innate sense of what seems like the best thing to do will always win the day. A smile, an apology, a compliment, sincerity, the desire to do what is right—any of these will smooth over a faux pas and leave others with a good impression of your character.

So step out. Have fun. Be considerate and kind, and you'll do nothing to spoil the fun of others.

Theater, Concerts, and Movies

Your seats are located in the center of a row in which others are already seated. You have options in maneuvering past them to get to your seat: you can turn and face them, which allows for eye contact, always helpful as you inconvenience them; or you can present your posterior to their faces and avoid the withering glance that is being directed your way. Either way, be sure to say "Excuse me." If you have season tickets on the inside of a row, the considerate thing to do would be to arrive early.

When the lights go out and the show starts, it's amazing how some people talk out loud, put their feet on seats, play with their smartphones, and display all manner of inconsiderate behavior.

Being out in public is not the same as being in your living room. Responsible behavior is, or should be, the norm. It shouldn't be up to theater management to have to remind people to turn off the electronics, yet even the most well-mannered audience member may occasionally forget to do this. There's nothing more distracting to a performer than to have to compete with a tinny, seemingly endless ringtone. What's even worse are the loud protestations by the audience surrounding the offender, who all too often has to fumble through a variety of pockets or an oversized handbag to locate the culprit device.

Wouldn't it be safer simply to leave your smartphone home when you go out? Consider whether you could do without it for a few hours. Perhaps theaters should declare themselves cell-phone-free and well as smoke-free zones.

BONUS POINTS

You were almost at the theater when your son called to tell you he was sick and heading off to the student health office. You decide to proceed as planned anyway, but suspect that you may be receiving a call during the show. You should alert those around you that you might have to leave your seat. If your seat is not on the aisle, ask if you could switch seats so as not to inconvenience others. Be sure to set your phone to vibrate.

Remember that most theaters, like airplanes, are not configured with two armrests per seat. It's possible to share an armrest with a complete stranger, if each of you is careful and try not to elbow the other out of the way.

Open your candy before the lights go down; crackling wrappers are very distracting to others. So is frequent coughing. Bring some cough drops along just in case you get a tickle in your throat; consider offering one to a neighbor who repeatedly coughs or clears her throat. Don't slurp your soda loudly, or chew ice with your mouth open.

Consider the people seated around you. You may have dressed up for the occasion, but your designer hat will need to come off so that the person behind you can see. Remember that scents, whether colognes or perfumes, can be irritating to others, so minimize their usage.

There are concerts and there are concerts. Behavior at a rock concert is pretty much anything goes. The crowd expects to be standing up, clapping, singing along, dancing, whistling, and yelling out requests. The joint will be jumping, and the volume will be pumped up. (You might want to bring some earplugs along to protect what's left of your hearing.)

If some of the people around you are particularly bothersome, you may need to get an usher to ensure acceptable behavior. It's usually not a good idea to try to enforce better behavior yourself, even if you're bigger than the other person.

A symphony concert is a different story. For example, you can turn around, and quietly ask the woman behind you to kindly stop jolting the back of your seat with her knees. Say it with a smile. Mind that your coat is not hanging way over the back of your seat. Put your program down at your feet, to be sure that it won't fall off your lap during the *andante cantabile*.

It should go without saying, but it's not polite to go to the bathroom during the show. Use the facilities before curtain time.

This usually means arriving at the theater in plenty of time. And why not? You got all dressed up. Give others a chance to see you parading around the lobby in your finery!

Sporting Events

Sporting events engender some truly awful behavior. All too often the game seems to be incidental to consuming as much beer as is physically possible, which means a constant parade back and forth—to the bar, to the bathroom, to the exit ramp for a smoke, and so on. And the language that's used will be colorful, to say the least.

If you're bringing the kids, see whether the venue features a family section. Point out examples of bad behavior, so that your children don't grow up perpetuating boorishness. Teach them that it's okay to cheer something well done by the visiting team. Again, let the usher know if someone in your section is out of line; you're not in a position to be the rule enforcer. You can always ask to be moved to a different seat.

Set a good example; if you have to get up and squeeze past others, say "Excuse me." Don't just stand there until they notice you and get up to let you by. And say "Thank you" as you pass through, both ways.

When somebody in front of you repeatedly jumps up, obscuring your vision, you might say, "It's hard to see when you're standing. I'd appreciate it if you could stay in your seat until the play is over."

Restaurants and Happy Hours

If you're planning to eat at a popular spot, be sure to call ahead and make a reservation. If for any reason your plans change, have the courtesy to notify the establishment that you are canceling.

When the restaurant is crowded and space is limited, be sure to check your coat if possible. When you retrieve your belongings, tip the attendant $2 per item.

If you're at a swanky joint and you want a front-row table—for example, to see the floor show—you'll need to tip the maitre d'. Depending upon where you are, the amount you tip may be as high as $50. Fold your bill into a small square with the denomination showing, and slip it subtly into the maitre d's palm. Practice this with your significant other a few times at home, so you'll be able to do it smoothly.

If you've invited others to join you at a restaurant, you have in effect become the host, even if the plan is to go Dutch treat. Be sure to get there early. Getting together for happy hour is much less formal—sort of like the difference between going on a date and just hanging out.

Happy hour is all about drinking, and the bar menu is more or less incidental to the booze. The noise level is high, the ambience low. The more you drink, the less you'll care. Still, you want to preserve at least a modicum of decorum. Avoid provoking people who have been drinking. If you're traveling by car, select a designated driver. If that person abrogates her responsibility and nobody else is in condition to drive safely, call a cab, or have a friend swing by and drive you home.

Museums, Churches, and Galleries

Patience, patience, patience. You really want to see the museum's newly acquired Van Gogh, but so does everyone else. Wait your turn. Don't cut in front of the little old lady trying to read the story behind the painting. Some people move across the room from right to left, while others go the other way. A museum, and especially a gallery, is not run like Disneyland. If you bump into somebody, by now you should know what to say, and how to say it. If someone bumps into you, try not to take it personally.

Allow yourself plenty of time. This isn't about "doing the Louvre" in two hours—you'll just annoy others with your impatience. A big museum is an all-day affair. Have lunch there. Sit down frequently and take time to process what you've seen. Perhaps you don't get to see the thirteenth-century armament collection—now you have a reason to come back. If you rush through the place, it all becomes a blur.

You don't need to reach out and touch the marble just because the guard happens to be looking the other way. Respect these treasures; there are monuments in the park you can hang from, or climb upon, if that is your thing.

Remember that museums are quiet places. Keep your cell phone off when going through the galleries. Avoid making insensitive or offensive comments out loud, such as, "If you've seen one fresco, you've seen them all."

Be especially respectful in churches. Whatever your belief system may be, a church is a holy place—if not for you, for others. Don't discard gum wrappers into holy water fonts; don't take flash photographs where signs expressly disallow the practice. Talk in a whisper, if you must talk at all, and dress appropriately.

At the Gym

If you're ill, stay away from the gym. There are enough germs going around without adding yours to the party. Make use of the hand-sanitizer dispenser on your way in and out. And wipe off the equipment after you use it. Be sure not to hog the treadmill; most gyms have a 20- or 30-minute limit. If somebody beats you to your favorite aerobic machine and you don't have time to wait until she's finished, try something else.

Never drop the heavy weights; ask someone to spot you if you're pushing your limits. Keep the grunts and groans to a minimum, and don't count your reps out loud, because this could throw others off their routine. Put the weights back where they belong when you're done.

Be on time to your gym class. If you're late, come in as quietly as possible; the rest of the class doesn't need to know that you've arrived. If you need to leave early, try to inform the teacher before the class starts, and exit respectfully, which means quietly.

Respect for others can take many forms at the gym. Stow your gear out of the way; don't leave it out where a person could trip over it. Turn off the cell phone so as not to disturb others. Respect your neighbor's space—don't walk on her yoga mat, for example. Avoid crowding wherever possible.

If you need to leave the class to use the facilities, go and return quietly. You'll greatly reduce the likelihood of this happening if you arrive at the gym early enough to do your business beforehand.

Make sure your workout gear is always clean; don't let it marinate inside your gym locker. Body odor can be equally pervasive. Certainly your postworkout shower will get rid of it, but don't make your fellow gym members have to wait until then—apply deodorant before your workout.

Shopping

Keep reminding yourself to be patient. Your sales clerk may be irritatingly slow, but she's the one you are working with, unless you want to walk all the way down to the register at the other end of the store, where the lines may be longer and the clerk even slower. If you try to rush the salesperson, she may make a mistake in the transaction that will cost you more time in the long run.

Sales can be especially trying, as everyone is rushing to grab up the latest iPhone. It's not the end of the world if you don't get one today. Keep things in perspective. You'll stay healthy longer, and you'll live to see many more smartphone innovations.

Shopping can test your patience in any number of ways, but there are solutions. Finding an empty changing room on a crowded day can be a challenging experience; perhaps you should do your shopping at off-peak hours. Stores' return policies vary; some are downright irritating. Instead of making a scene with the clerk, you might consider asking for the manager. Explaining your situation calmly and politely to someone in a position to bend the rules a bit may make all the difference.

MISERABLE MOMENTS

You snag a parking spot in a crowded lot. In your haste, you open your car door, and it smacks into the car next to you. Ouch. It leaves a dent.

What to do? Leave a note under the windshield wiper with your name and contact information. Write "Sorry!" on it, especially if you're leaving a business card. While the temptation to run might be strong, you're probably on candid camera anyway, which is another reason to do the right thing.

Malls present particular problems. Parking lot rudeness is common. Much of this will be avoided if you're willing to park at some distance and walk a bit to where you're going.

Courtesy for the Disabled

Chapter 11

Disabled people are just like you or me. In fact, disabilities affect one out of every five Americans. Some are partial, some are total; some are obvious, some are subtle.

Those who are affected may have been so for some time, possibly from birth. Others have only lately developed their disability. Many hold important jobs; some are homeless and unemployed. Quite a number of people have become so self-sufficient, even in the face of severe disability, that they require little or no assistance. Depending upon the way the offer for assistance is made, it may be gratefully accepted, or it may be peremptorily declined.

The disabled are made uncomfortable all too often by the lack of accommodation for their particular needs. Don't make things worse for them by staring or making inappropriate remarks. Indeed, you may well be more self-conscious than necessary around a person who is disabled; once again, respect, consideration, and kindness will win the day.

Physical Disabilities

Physical disabilities come in many varieties, yet most don't preclude relatively normal activities, including gainful employment, often in positions of great responsibility. The Americans with Disabilities Act has helped a great many people reach their full potential. And in turn, these influential and admirable individuals have been instrumental in alerting the nondisabled to the fact that those who have impairments are otherwise normal. And they want and deserve to be treated that way.

Mobility Impairment

The ambulatory aid deserves the same respect as the person using it; regard it as a personal space expander. If the person who's disabled moves or is moved from a wheelchair to a stationary chair or bed, keep the wheelchair within sight and easy reach, in case the person wants to go back to it. The same goes for walkers, canes, or crutches. Don't take these aids away and stow them in a closet, leaving the dependent person helpless (unless that's the point, as in cases of Alzheimer's).

If you're carrying on a conversation with a wheelchair-bound person, be sure to sit yourself. Keep the discussion on an eye-to-eye level to avoid the appearance of superiority or the fact that you're healthy and have no need for a wheelchair.

Don't be condescending if you're offering to push the wheelchair across the street or up the hill. Be matter of fact. Give the person to whom you're offering assistance a way out. Say something like, "I see that this hill is getting rather steep. Would you like me to give you a hand getting to the top?"

If the offer is refused, you might follow with, "Let me know if you change your mind. I'm going that way myself." If accepted, make a little pleasant conversation while you push, assuming you aren't too out of breath from the exertion.

Doors are particularly challenging for a person who is mobility impaired. Say something in a matter-of-fact way, such as, "This door is kind of heavy. Let me give you a hand." This is a much better way to put it than, say, "Do you need a hand here?"

BONUS POINTS

The opportunity for you to offer your seat on the bus to a person with a cane may present itself, but don't force the issue. The person justly may be proud that he can stand up and hold on to a strap like everyone else.

If you're the one who's disabled and on the receiving side of the offer, yet you prefer to remain standing, don't be curt in your refusal; smile and decline gracefully, perhaps adding something like, "Standing for a certain length of time like this is good for me."

If you have a recent disability and you're invited to a function by someone who's unaware of your condition, be sure to let him know, so that any necessary accommodation can be provided.

It's perfectly fine to compliment a person on his beautifully made cane or brand-new silastic seat cushion. You would do this in the same way you would admire a person's raincoat.

MISERABLE MOMENTS

You see a person park in a disabled parking spot and hop out of the car like a cheerleader about to turn a cartwheel. He's not even using a cane.

Don't assume he's bogus. He may be wearing an artificial limb. You're not a meter maid; you're probably not a doctor (in any case, you aren't *his* doctor); you aren't even a concerned citizen; you're disgruntled because you had to park farther away. This is your problem, not his. Don't attempt a confrontation.

Obesity

Being a bit overweight doesn't constitute a disability. Obesity is defined by a body mass index (or BMI—the ratio of weight divided by height squared) of greater than 30. More than 1 out of every 30 Americans now falls into this category. Crossing that threshold still doesn't qualify a person for disability status.

However, associated medical conditions will become more evident at the higher levels of BMI, especially as a person ages. So-called medical comorbidities such as diabetes, high blood pressure, arthritis, congestive heart failure, and sleep apnea will tip the balance into zones of partial or even complete disability. Most authorities consider morbid obesity, which is a person with BMI greater than 40, a disability, with or without any demonstrable comorbidities.

Morbidly obese individuals suffer from severe discrimination. People look askance when they order food; bystanders snicker behind their backs as they walk down the street. Many people consider severe obesity as a lack of will power, not as the disease that it is. There are remedies, such as gastric bypass, but these remedies aren't without serious risk, and they're costly. Many who would benefit from surgical intervention are afraid to take a chance that they might have serious complications; some are too unhealthy to even be considered as surgical candidates.

If you're overweight, you know to look out for stronger chairs, reinforced toilets, and gates rather than turnstiles. You may choose to opt out of swimming parties. You know how cruel people can be, often unintentionally.

If you're inviting an oversized person to a function, as a host you'll want to make sure there's an armless seating option or wider seat availability, and not too far a walk or too many stairs.

Sensory Disabilities

There are many degrees of hearing impairment. Some hearing-impaired people are totally deaf, yet are so facile at lip-reading that their deficit is nearly undetectable to the average observer, so long as the lips of that average observer remain within their line of vision.

Similarly, you can't always tell if a person is visually impaired. They may have partial vision. They may be wearing dark glasses. Indeed, they may be so used to the route they're taking that familiarity, plus a heightening of their other senses, will give them an appearance of one who sees reasonably well.

Hearing Loss and Speaking Impairments

A hearing aid may help most but not all of those who are hearing impaired. And those tiny little batteries may run down at the most inopportune moments, when replacement batteries might not be readily at hand. Contrary to what you might think, difficulty hearing is not always associated with speaking problems; each has multiple causes and variable manifestations.

Signing is now being offered in many schools as a "foreign language substitute"; as a result, more people "speak" it. At the same time, those who are hearing impaired to the point where hearing aids make little or no difference are almost always good lip readers.

Don't overexaggerate your words; don't duck your head down or cover your mouth; make sure the lighting is adequate. Start the conversation by saying the name of the person who is hearing impaired to get his attention, or tap him lightly on the shoulder. If necessary, a small wave of the hand should work.

When the conversation starts, avoid shouting. Never attempt to converse with gum or food in your mouth; these affect the way your lips move in speech. Speak slowly, without dropping your voice at the end of each sentence in cases where the person to whom you're speaking has partial hearing. Pause at the end of each phrase before going on, to make sure you have been fully understood. If you aren't understood, you can repeat what you said; if this doesn't work, you'll want to rephrase your comments.

There are times, though, when paper and pen will be required. This is the slowest yet surest way of making certain the two of you understand each other fully. Have patience, whether you're the speaker or the one spoken to.

People with speaking impairments may or may not also have hearing deficits, yet communication still can proceed. Often, as you spend more time with a person and give that person your full concentration, you'll better understand him. If you're in a crowded or noisy environment, you may want to suggest that the two of you move to a quieter place.

Allow the person with whom you're speaking plenty of time to say what he has to say. Don't blithely nod your head as if to say you understand when you don't. Stop the person by raising your hand and ask for clarification. Focus on listening to the words and not to the way they're spoken. If some words are mispronounced, let it go.

Say what you have to say to a person who is hearing or speaking impaired face-to-face wherever possible. Despite amplification devices for phones, people with these disabilities usually prefer not to talk on the phone any more than they have to. Texting works much better. And don't worry; the person who's hearing impaired will have his phone set to vibrate, so your message will not go ignored.

Visual Impairment

There's no shame in offering to help and having your offer declined; the person who's visually impaired may in fact be unsure if there's anyone around in a position to help him. Ask matter-of-factly if you can be of any assistance, perhaps with a visibility-neutral comment such as, "It's so hard to reach anything in this market. I have long arms. Might I be of assistance?"

If the person with visual impairment is heading straight for a wall covered with fresh paint, you'll want to be more forceful, with a firm comment like, "I'm steering you away from a freshly painted wall. I hope you don't mind my intervention."

In assisting with ambulation, as in crossing a difficult intersection, offer your arm and let the person you're helping take it. Don't take his arm. He will be easily able to follow you if he is holding your arm; if you're holding on to him, you'll need to steer him. Steering is more difficult for the person who's impaired visually.

Persons who are visually impaired will sometimes be accompanied by a guide dog, often referred to as a Seeing Eye dog. You'll be able to distinguish these working dogs from your average pooch by the harness they wear. Don't distract them from their duty in any way: no petting, no treats, no speaking at all to the dog without permission of its owner. And don't let your dog get too close to the guide dog.

You'll need to think before giving directions. Telling a person who can't see to "take a right when you get to Main Street" won't work. Rather tell him to "turn right after walking straight ahead for three blocks." If he has partial vision, or is used to using a cane, he'll be good to go.

If you step into a room with a person who is unable to see, make sure to set him at ease by immediately identifying yourself. If you're there with others, say something like, "It's Emily here, and Katie is on my right." The person you're addressing may not see the hand you advance to shake, so you may want to say, "It's been a while since I saw you. Let's shake hands." When the person who is sight impaired advances his hand, and the direction might be a bit off, take it and make him feel comfortable and welcome. Be sure to excuse yourself before leaving.

Mental Disabilities

Mental disabilities vary in kind and severity. Some are temporary; others are permanent; some are present from birth; others occur later. Some are associated with altered perception of reality. Some are only noticeable in times of stress.

The best thing you can do in general is to treat such people as normally as possible. Above all, be patient.

Being around those who have mental disabilities can be extremely challenging. Some conditions make those who are unaffected quite uncomfortable. Try not to exhibit any apprehensions you may have. Staying calm will be reassuring to most people with these conditions, even the most severely affected. Keep an even, pleasant tone in your voice and a smile on your face.

Caring for a loved one who's going through the stages of progressive dementia can be an almost overwhelming challenge, both physically and emotionally. Books such as *The 36-Hour Day: A Family Guide to Caring for Persons with Alzheimer Disease* provide essential support.

Keep in mind that with progressive dementia, there will come a time when your own parent no longer recognizes you. He may seem to be talking to someone who isn't there. Heartbreaking as it is, realize that this is the nature of this disease. Gently try to coax your father back to reality. He may remember a trip to the racetrack or seeing Babe Ruth. He may respond to having his hair combed or a gentle, loving massage. Cherish the happy memories, while you make him as comfortable as you can.

The Circle of Life

Births, christenings, coming-of-age ceremonies, birthdays, retirements, engagements, weddings, funerals. These are the milestones of our lives. Each milestone represents one door closing and another door opening. Each is a time of community, a time when we depend on each other to share our excitement, our joy, our anxiety, our sadness. Each is a time to support one another.

We all depend on each other and take comfort in the goodwill we extend one another. The best way to do this is to celebrate key events in each others' lives. The arrival of children and their maturation along with weddings, retirements, funerals, and similar events are surrounded by and enriched by tradition and ceremony, some of it joyful, some somber. Appropriate and considerate behavior on these occasions is always much appreciated and long remembered.

Beginning with Babies

Birth announcements frequently take the form of printed cards or emails. These announcements should include the baby's full name and date of birth, and parents' names. Options would include height and weight and a photograph. Although receiving such an announcement is a cause for joy and a reason for response, gift giving is optional.

Christenings

Most likely, invitations to a christening party are the first in the cycle of life. Usually baptism occurs within six weeks of birth, and sometimes within the first two weeks, in the Catholic faith. Among Protestants, baptism generally occurs within six months, although it's not unusual to have the ceremony later than that. Those who convert to a faith later in life go through the same ceremony that a baby does, except that they can choose their own godparents, and they can respond to the ceremony's questions themselves.

Very often, the religious ceremony is followed by a party. Traditionally, christening parties are small, although they're gaining in popularity, size, and elaborateness. If you're invited, bring a small gift.

If you're asked to be a godparent, remember that this is a high honor involving serious responsibilities. The godparents are expected to oversee the spiritual education of the child, particularly if the parents are deceased. Sometimes godparents become legal guardians of the child if the parents die.

Godparents may give a joint gift or separate gifts, and gifts to the child can take the form of a savings account in the child's name, or some larger object such as a stroller or even an entire layette, especially if the parents are going through difficult financial times. Otherwise, typical mementos are a silver rattle, cup, picture frame, or similar keepsake.

The form of reception or party following the christening service may depend on the time of day. If it's a morning service, there may be an informal light lunch. An early afternoon service can be followed by a tea party, and a late-afternoon service can be followed by a champagne-and-cocktails party.

Invitations are by telephone, email, evite, or note, but the parents may want to have printed invitations so that they can keep them as souvenirs.

Typically the baby is attired in a long white gown or christening dress, which often is a family heirloom. The highlight of the party is cutting the christening cake (white with white icing and the baby's name or birth date in frosting) by the parents and a toast offered by the godparents. Then any others who have a serious, sentimental, or amusing thought may propose their own toasts to the new member of the family.

Brit

A Jewish boy is circumcised eight days after birth and is given a Hebrew name at the Brit Milah (covenant of circumcision) ceremony. This may take place at home, hospital, or synagogue; it may be an intimate event with family members and friends or a celebration open to the community.

A Jewish girl may be given her name on the eighth day after birth or on another day during a service at synagogue or at a ceremony at home. A special blessing that includes the girl's name is recited and a modest celebration of the Brit Bat (covenant of a daughter) may follow.

First Communion

When a Catholic child reaches the age of 7 or so and receives communion for the first time, it's often an occasion for a family party as well as a religious ceremony. The girls wear pretty white dresses, sometimes with veils, and the boys wear blue or gray suits. If you aren't Catholic, you shouldn't receive communion. Sometimes a breakfast or brunch follows the ceremony. Appropriate gifts include a prayer book or some other religious item.

Birthdays

Birthday parties can take many forms, informal and formal. Sometimes they're very structured events to celebrate milestone birthdays. Other times they're low-key events that serve as a good excuse to bring family and friends together for a celebration. The main thing to remember is to participate in whatever way you're asked, and to respond to the invitation quickly. Don't plan a surprise gag without first asking the host. Not everybody shares the same sense of humor.

Joking about someone's age is best left to the birthday celebrant herself. Many people are very sensitive about growing older, so prank cards and comments about age can hurt rather than help. Forget about sending snarky cards, too. They might be funny, yet that knife can cut both ways. Instead, celebrate someone's life. Let the celebrants know that their birthday is a reason to tell them how glad and grateful you are to be a part of their life.

Coming-of-Age Events

Most cultures celebrate "coming of age." While the intent is more or less the same, the celebrations themselves are diverse and culturally rich. It's considered rude to show up for the party and skip the religious ceremony, unless your invitation clearly states the time and place of the party, with no mention of the ceremony itself.

Confirmation

This usually is a quiet family occasion, when a child officially becomes a member of the congregation at the age of 12 or 13.

Usually only family members and godparents attend the ceremony and the gathering afterward. Simple, religious gifts are appropriate. Children wear their "Sunday best" clothes, but veils are not generally worn.

Bar and Bat Mitzvah

During his bar mitzvah, the 13-year-old boy, having studied the Talmud and recited the lesson in Hebrew, is told, "You're now entering the Congregation of Israel." It's one of the most important ceremonies in the life of a Jewish man. In Reform congregations, there's a similar ceremony for 13-year-old girls, called bat or bas mitzvah.

The ceremony itself is impressive. It can last three hours in an Orthodox temple, about half that time in a Conservative temple, and about an hour in a Reform temple. Often a lavish party follows the ceremony.

Don't send or bring gifts to the temple. It's preferable to send the gifts to the home rather than take them to the party.

At one time, it was traditional to give a fountain pen for a bar mitzvah gift. Gifts of money are appropriate, yet a gift that reinforces the Jewish faith and traditions is more meaningful. For example, subscriptions from The Jewish Publication Society (jewishpub.org) can provide a year of faith-based writings.

The *Quinceanera*

This coming-of-age celebration is one of the biggest occasions in a young Latina's life. Often called a *quince*, meaning "fifteen," the event is planned for and talked about within the family almost as enthusiastically as a wedding. Frequently, a religious ceremony precedes the party. The young girl wears a white gown and sometimes borrows a special piece of jewelry from a relative to wear at her celebration.

The party takes the form of a miniball and guests typically dress formally. Music is an important part of the celebration, and the celebrant's father dances the first waltz with her. After that, guests join the dancing. Gifts, usually checks or jewelry, should not be brought to the party, but rather sent to the girl's home.

Nuptials

This section is intended to give you an idea of what to expect when you're a wedding guest or part of the wedding party. It's not a wedding planning guide.

Before the Wedding

Traditionally engagement parties were small events, usually a cocktail party hosted by a godparent, grandparents, or very close friends. In the days when engagements were at least a year long, the engagement party was the first time the bride-to-be wore her engagement ring in public.

Engagement presents are no longer common customs. Friends of the couple rarely, if ever, give engagement gifts. Occasionally older relatives do, and those gifts typically are personal in nature, such as a piece of heirloom jewelry.

It's not appropriate for the bride's mother or sister to host the bridal shower. This should be done by the friends of the bride. Coed showers are common today, such as a cocktail party or barbecue. More than one shower from both sides of the family is over the top. Remember that everyone who's invited to the shower should be invited to the wedding, and that means giving a gift for each. Gifts typically should be useful for the couple's new life, such as housewares or gardening gear. If you know the couple could use a monetary gift, be sure to present it in a tasteful card.

All-girl showers usually are held at lunchtime or during the day. Often they include customs such as making a fake bridal bouquet from the bows on the packages, which is then used for the church rehearsal.

The Wedding—Who Pays for What

When it comes to the wedding process, there is always the question of who pays for what. For many weddings, lots of people assume a share of the burden and thus have some say in the proceedings.

Traditionally, the bride's family pays for invitations, announcements, photographs at the wedding and reception, flowers for the wedding party, the cost of the ceremony itself (flowers, canopy, music, cars, and so on), and all the reception expenses.

The groom is responsible for the marriage license, the bride's ring, his gift to the bride, the officiant's fee, gifts for his attendants, and the honeymoon. Sometimes the groom pays for the bride's bouquet, the corsages for the mothers and grandmothers, and the boutonnieres for his attendants and the fathers. The groom's family pays for the rehearsal dinner and hotel accommodations for the groom and his attendants.

But tradition aside, the most practical and workable way to allocate wedding expenses is for the bride, the groom, and their families to sit down together and discuss the costs openly. This way, everyone will have the same picture of the event in his or her mind. Clear communication is essential from the start, especially about who should be billed for what as well as billing and payment procedures.

The wedding guest list determines the cost and size of the wedding, so it's a good idea to agree on some outer limits before you begin. Usually the two families—the bride's and the groom's—decide the number of guests equally between them.

Because so many couples are waiting to get married until they are well into their careers, it's common for the couple to pay for their own wedding. That means that they get to make the rules.

Couples marrying beyond the first time are expected to pay for all their own wedding expenses, and to make the wedding considerably more modest than the first one.

The bride's and groom's attendants pay for their own wedding attire and transportation to and from the wedding. They also pay their portion of the bridesmaids' and groomsmen's group gifts to the newlyweds.

The Wedding Party—Who Does What

The bride's attendants include all the bridesmaids, the matron of honor (personally, I prefer to rename this the lady-in-waiting because it was hard to accept being called a matron when I served at my best friend's wedding after I was married), maid of honor, junior bridesmaid, ring bearer, and flower girl (or two). Some couples are now imitating European weddings and having several little girls as attendants rather than bridesmaids, in addition to the maid of honor. More than six attendants is reminiscent of a chorus line and runs the risk of robbing the bride of all the attention due her. Only one attendant is absolutely necessary, and it doesn't matter whether she's single or married. The bride's attendants should be close to her in age and either close friends or siblings.

Although it isn't mandatory for the bridesmaids to give the bride a party prior to the wedding, this is a lovely tradition. The maid of honor should organize it, together with the matron of honor if there is one. Usually it's held the same night as the groom's bachelor party. It's up to the lead attendant to organize the gift from the attendants, purchase it, and collect the money, as well as monogramming or engraving if that is required. She also would run errands for the bride before the wedding and help her to get dressed for the wedding. Bridesmaids should make sure that the wedding dress and veil are returned to the bride's home safely after the reception if the bride and groom leave for a honeymoon directly from the wedding. Perhaps the biggest and most important job of the bridal attendants is to mingle with the other guests and make everyone feel welcome and comfortable. The bride should clue her attendants in as to wedding gift preferences so that they can inform guests who might ask them.

The best man is, in many ways, the unsung wedding hero. He is the only honor attendant for the groom. Frequently the groom's father assumes that role, or the groom's brother or best friend.

The best man needs to be a good manager as well as socially savvy and gregarious. It's his job to make sure that the ushers know what to wear, what to do, and when to do it. The best man is the go-to person when any of the bridesmaids needs help, when a wedding guest becomes drunk and unruly, or when the bar is running low and needs replenishing.

The best man organizes the bachelor dinner and his gift from the ushers and himself, and makes sure that the groom gets home safely afterward. The groom's gift to the ushers and their joint gift to him are exchanged at the bachelor dinner. At the wedding, the best man makes sure that the groomsmen have their wedding ties and boutonnieres in place. He also makes sure that he and the groom get to the church on time—at least half an hour before the start of the ceremony.

The first toast at both the rehearsal dinner and the wedding come from the best man. It's his job to determine the order of the toasts, which should be planned in advance. That means he invites certain guests to make toasts to the couple before the wedding day so that they can prepare their remarks. He also corrals the wedding party for the official photographs, which usually happens at the reception just before the guests begin arriving. If the newlyweds are leaving on a honeymoon from the reception, the best man makes sure that the travel documents are in order and gives them to the groom as they are leaving. He's also responsible for transportation from the reception to the airport, if that's needed, and taking charge of the couple's luggage before they embark.

Ushers usually are the same age as the groom, and most often are brothers of the groom and bride, or close friends. Their main duty is to seat guests at the ceremony. Each usher escorts as many ladies up the aisle as he can. All guests are greeted and asked if they are friends of the bride or the groom. An usher offers his inside arm to the lady. When more than one woman arrive together, he escorts the most senior of them, and the rest follow. If a man and woman come to the ceremony together, the usher escorts the lady, and her male companion follows behind them.

Front pews are saved for members of the wedding party and families of the bride and groom. The bride's family sits on the left side, and the groom's family sits on the right. If there's an obviously unequal number of guests on one side or another, the ushers take it upon themselves to balance the group on either side.

For a daytime wedding during the winter, men should wear a dark suit with a dress shirt and tie, and dark shoes and socks. In the summer daytime, they should wear a lightweight dark suit with the same accessories as for a winter wedding. When the wedding is at a summer resort during the day, navy blue blazers with neutral-colored trousers would be appropriate, as are summer suits made of linen, poplin, or other lightweight fabric. Khaki trousers and jeans are too informal. If the wedding is very informal, such as on the beach, men should wear a summer sports coat with white or contrasting color trousers.

"Black-tie" invitations require a tuxedo with a white or cream dress shirt. Pleated shirts are fine, but leave the ruffled shirts for your high school prom. Dress shirts mean cuff links. Black socks and black leather shoes complete the outfit. Colored ties and cummerbunds are fine, yet black is always best. Black-tie weddings only occur at 6 o'clock or later.

BONUS POINTS

At Jewish services, men typically wear a yarmulke on their head. They will be provided outside the sanctuary. Women cover their heads for some Conservative services. Frequently there will be something provided for women, such as a handkerchief, at special celebrations. Prayer shawls are only for Jewish people of the congregation, although they might be outside the sanctuary as well. It's disrespectful to flaunt religious symbols or jewelry of a different faith when you're a guest in someone's place of worship.

Destination Weddings

Destination weddings often sound more romantic than they actually are when it comes to the logistics. Usually a save-the-date announcement is sent months in advance so that guests can clear their calendars, plan travel, and budget for the trip.

The upside of destination weddings is that they provide a picture-perfect setting and escape from daily chores, as well as an opportunity to visit with old friends and make new ones. The downside is that they're expensive in terms of time and money, and last-minute cancellation of plans can be costly. Guests are responsible for their own travel and lodging expenses, as well as giving a wedding gift. The gift doesn't need to be as elaborate as it might be for a traditional wedding, since the guest already incurs much expense just to show up.

Different Types of Wedding Ceremonies

In some ways, all weddings are the same. In other ways, they may be profoundly different. The following are some examples of different sorts of weddings and some ideas about what to expect.

Civil ceremonies are usually small. The only people who must be present for a civil ceremony are the bride and groom, the civil official, and the legal witnesses who need not even know the couple. Beyond that, the couple may be attended by a bridesmaid or bridesmaids, best man, groomsmen, maid or matron of honor, someone to give the bride away, ushers, possibly child attendants (flower girls or ring bearers), friends, and relatives.

Roman Catholics are married in the presence of a priest. They may or may not have a nuptial Mass. The bride's father walks the bride down the aisle and "gives" her to the groom, who walks out a few steps to meet her. The father then assumes his seat in the front pew on the left.

If a nuptial Mass takes place, the bride and groom and the wedding party receive Communion, and the guests frequently do as well. Of course, guests who are not of the faith will remain in their pews during Communion. That little bench at your feet is a kneeler, used during prayer; it's not a footrest. Family members or close friends often give scriptural readings.

Jewish wedding ceremonies vary from Orthodox to Reform. However, some components of the wedding service are found in all Jewish services.

The chuppah, or wedding canopy, covers the bride, groom, and rabbi during the ceremony. Originally, the chuppah was the bridal chamber itself. Today, the word symbolizes the couple's entering into the chamber.

In a traditional Jewish wedding ceremony, both the bride's mother and father give her away, not the father alone. The father is on one side, the mother on the other. Usually, both sets of parents stand just outside the canopy, not with the rest of the audience.

The wedding ring must be plain gold without any stones. The groom places it on the bride's finger as he says, "You are sanctified to me with this ring according to the religion of Moses and Israel." He and the bride sip wine from the same glass over which blessings have been said. The groom steps on the wine glass, crushing it, to symbolize Jewish mourning for the destruction of the Temple in ancient Jerusalem. The wine glass is covered with cloth before it's crushed to prevent splinters and cuts.

Jewish weddings are forbidden on holy days, such as the Sabbath. However, the holy days end at sundown, and many Jewish couples have Saturday-night weddings. Men cover their heads in the synagogue as a sign of respect for God. Guests are given yarmulkes for this purpose.

Generally, Islamic weddings aren't elaborate. The bride and groom exchange their vows in the mosque in the presence of family, friends, and the Imam, or religious leader. There are no restrictions as to color of clothing, but modest clothing is expected. Everyone removes their shoes before entering and places them on racks. Shoe removal is not a religious custom, but a sanitary one, since worshippers often pray touching the floor. At the end of the ceremony, those present often say *"Salaam aleikum"* ("Peace be with you") to one another.

After the ceremony, a reception is generally held in a hotel or hall. These receptions are very much like wedding receptions anywhere except that no alcohol is served and the food conforms to Islamic dietary laws.

Quaker weddings are warm, personal, and intimate. No clergy preside at Quaker weddings because Quakers believe that the divine spirit is present in all of us, and that we all are ministers, in a sense.

Guests enter the meetinghouse and sit wherever they feel comfortable. When all are seated, one person will stand and explain what to expect during the service. There will then be a period of silence, perhaps lasting several minutes. When they're ready, the bride and groom stand and exchange their vows. They then sit down, and another period of silence ensues.

After this period of silence, those present may rise and give their blessings to the couple. When the blessings are finished, the same person who spoke at the beginning of the meeting will "break" the meeting by rising and shaking the hand of someone nearby.

After the wedding, those present are invited to sign the marriage certificate. You need not be a Quaker to sign the certificate.

A bride or a groom who's a member of the armed forces may opt to be married in uniform. When either or both are in full dress uniform, it automatically adds formality to the ceremony. A non-military spouse-to-be would wear dignified apparel in order to show appropriate respect to the armed forces. Usually, the groom or bride's attendants are largely in uniform, although some of the ushers may be in civilian dress.

At the end of the ceremony, the ushers form the traditional "arch of steel," under which the bride and groom walk as they leave the ceremony. If the venue permits, the arch may be formed immediately after the bride and groom turn to face the assembled guests inside the building. In this case, the head usher calls "Center face," and the ushers form two lines facing each other on the steps beneath the altar. The next command is "Draw swords" or "Arch saber," and the ushers raise their swords, cutting edge facing up. The bride and groom pass under the arch.

The attendants then leave with the bride and groom. However, the attendants walk down the aisle and then leave through a side entrance to reassemble outside the building to form another arch. Other members in the wedding party wait just inside the building until the second arch is formed. Civilian ushers can choose to stand beside the military men forming the arch or not.

Same-Sex Weddings and Commitment Ceremonies

Gay couples who celebrate their commitment to each other often send formal invitations and invest as much energy into their ceremony as straight couples. Since the laws on gay marriages are constantly changing, you might be attending a commitment ceremony, rather than a legal marriage. It wouldn't be in good taste for you to ask at the reception, "So are you legally married?"

Often the couple dress alike for the ceremony—men might wear matching dark suits and women dress in the same color family and perhaps, style, carrying bouquets.

Even those guests who don't believe in the sanctity of these unions should attend to honor someone's lifetime commitment of love and respect—and participate, to the degree to which they're comfortable. If you're not sure how to address your friend's or relative's partner, ask in advance, "How do you want me to refer to Richard?"

Gift cards and letters of congratulations should express wishes for a long, happy, and abundant life together.

Retirement

When the retiree is someone you're friendly with, it's kind and gracious to commemorate the occasion. Be upbeat and focus on the future adventures in store. Many people are retiring earlier than the traditional age of 65, so retirement no longer is considered "being put out to pasture." Rather, emphasize what comes next—it might mean travel or even a whole new career.

Gifts are appropriate if you and the retiree are friends, and it's gracious to include the retiree's life partner in gifts—perhaps a gift certificate for a wonderful dinner. Retirees have the luxury of more time, so gifts that make time more enjoyable are welcome—for example, theater tickets, spa services, gardening tools, subscriptions to hobby magazines, gift certificates for a personal trainer, and so on.

If the retiree is the traditional age and has spent decades with one company, it's especially important not to patronize. It's a difficult time in the best of all worlds. Younger colleagues can create a real win-win when they take the time to get to know an older retiree and pick her brain about life and work. The retiree will feel valued, and the younger colleague will gain invaluable insights, information, and knowledge. Transitions are never easy, and retiring, in particular, should be treated with sensitivity. Forget sophomoric questions or jokes to spouses like "What will you do with each other every day?"

Funerals

The last rite of passage is the funeral. It's the most solemn, and a funeral warrants our most respectful behavior and dress. Friends and colleagues of the deceased should dress in simple, quiet clothing. Men should wear a jacket and tie, if not a suit. Family members of the deceased wear conservative attire, although the strictly black mourning costume is no longer necessarily observed.

Often a viewing or wake is held at a funeral home the day before the funeral, and sometimes for a short time prior to the actual funeral ceremony. Generally it's held in the early evening or late afternoon, so that people who are working can pay their respects to the bereaved family. The casket is present, which may be open or closed, and all the flowers sent to the funeral home are displayed. Sometimes there are picture collages of the deceased, especially when the casket is closed.

There's a guest book to sign, which becomes important to the family later as they process their grief. Sign the book, and indicate your connection to the deceased if you don't know the family. For example, "Howard and I were in Rotary Club together." It may be that you never knew the departed, yet you're there through your connection to a family member. You might write something like, "Although I never had the opportunity to meet Mae, I worked for years with Jon, and I know how close he was to his mother."

The viewing is a time when individuals who cannot attend the funeral itself can console the bereaved. The wake doesn't need to be formal with a receiving line unless the family prefers it. Generally when the deceased is very well known and large numbers of people are expected to attend, the family forms a receiving line. Everyone greets the bereaved and often exchange hugs and kisses as they speak brief, consoling words. For example, "I'm so sorry for your loss. We will miss Thomas." As uncomfortable as you might be talking with the bereaved, be assured that they'll remember the fact that you were there, and likely not recall the words you spoke. So don't be intimidated.

If you send flowers, they can go to the home of the bereaved, the funeral home, the church, or the gravesite. Include a card saying something like, "With deepest sympathy from the Hunter Family." The envelope should contain the name and postal address of the donor of the flowers. Some churches have strict rules about flowers, so check before sending flowers there. Don't send flowers to a Jewish or Muslim family.

Charity donations in the name of the deceased are always appreciated. Send the check directly to the charity, not the family, noting that it is "in memory of ...." The charity will notify the family of the donation.

Never presume to speak at a memorial service unless you're asked. If you're asked to speak, keep your remarks short. Praise the deceased. If possible, tell a humorous story reflecting the excellent character or good humor of the deceased. Write down your remarks in advance and practice. This is no time to ad lib or ramble. And be sure your electronic communication devices are turned off.

Giving and Receiving Gifts

Gifts have been part of life since the beginning of civilization. Both giving them and receiving them can bring joy, or confusion, or embarrassment. Probably you grew up hearing your mother say, "It's the thought that counts," when she was trying to get you to appreciate that ugly tie or sweater from Aunt Lillie. Yet sometimes gift giving can reflect lack of thought, and that creates problems.

You might not buy the adage that it's better to give than receive. Still, you must buy the fact that it's important to do both graciously. The art of gift giving doesn't come as naturally as most of us would like to think.

The very first question to ask yourself when you plan to give a gift should be, "Why am I giving it?" We give gifts to celebrate birthdays and holidays, to congratulate someone, to thank someone for a meal in his home or for taking us to a restaurant, in appreciation for valuable information or making contacts for us, for anniversaries. And those are just a few of the occasions.

Some Gift Guidelines

Thoughtfulness and generosity of spirit are the watchwords of giving gracefully. That doesn't mean you need unlimited funds. In fact, the only true gifts we can give are our time and our attention. They are priceless.

Once you've figured out why you're giving the gift in the first place, reflect for a moment on whether the gift is sincere and whether you're giving it with no strings attached. Otherwise, it's a payment for services rendered.

If you have any doubt that the gift is too extravagant, don't give it. An Asian adage, "Do not lead a man where he cannot follow" is a worthy guideline. In short, if you think for a moment that your gift will embarrass its receiver, who might not be able to reciprocate in kind, back off. Extravagance can be bad manners and bad strategy, especially in the work arena.

Gag gifts should be given very sparingly; not everybody will get the joke that strikes you funny. Ask yourself if the gift is appropriate. A box of chocolates for a pal who's dieting is both inconsiderate and borders on passive aggressive, just as giving a bottle of wine to a recovering alcoholic would be. Kindness is the mantra for any gift you give.

Ask yourself if your gift reflects the receiver's taste rather than your own. Ever wonder why we sometimes never see a person wearing that great scarf we gave them, or those fabulous earrings? Chances are you've chosen the scarf in your favorite color, without realizing that the color you've chosen makes the receiver look pallid at best.

Check with parents if you plan on giving their child a gift. What you might consider appropriate could be another parent's nightmare. Never, ever give pets as a gift.

The value of a gift is enhanced when it's beautifully wrapped and it arrives on time. Including a handwritten note makes the gift all the more special, even if you simply add a few lines to a greeting card.

Acknowledging Gifts

When you open a gift in front of the person who gave it to you, smile and enthusiastically thank him for thinking of you in such a lovely way. Never, ever make a comment that's sarcastic or negative, such as "I hope this fits," or "You really knocked yourself out with this one, didn't you?" You might have to bite your tongue, but so be it.

If you receive a gift in the mail, or the giver isn't otherwise present, always let the giver know that you received the gift. The thank-you note might be sent a day or so later, but whenever we send something, it's important to us to know that it got to the right place. Whenever we say thank you, we change someone's life a little bit. This is when the speed and immediacy of technology are our great allies. Follow up a quick notification with a handwritten thank-you note.

Even young children can draw a picture of the gift and print their name on a piece of paper, which you can send along to the giver. Let the child's imagination rule within the boundaries of good taste. What's key here is to make the thank-you project fun so that children look forward to sending thank-you notes as they mature.

What if the gift arrives and it's broken? No need to upset the person who sent the gift; thank the giver, and if it was sent by a store, let the store know that the gift arrived in bad condition. Most retailers will replace damaged or broken items, and it's likely that there's a return label included in the package. If the giver packed the gift himself and you think you can repair it easily, just do that. This is where it's the thought that counts.

To Regift, or Not to Regift?

Regifting is a fact of life, and someone who claims never to regift is likely guilty of a misstatement. We all receive things we can't use or just don't like. One person's found object can be another person's treasure. When you know that something truly will please another, go ahead and give it. Be certain, though, that you remove all prior wrappings and are very careful to remove any gift enclosure card. And don't be a cheapskate about rewrapping the regift. By wrapping it beautifully, you're lavishing your own time and attention on the other person, and that's a gift in itself.

MISERABLE MOMENTS

You just committed a serious faux pas: you regifted a present to the person who had previously given it to you! Red faces during the holidays should come from the weather, not gift-giving gaffes. This never would have happened had you kept a log of gifts given and received.

Admitting that you're regifting an item is not terrible. For instance, you might say to someone, "A colleague gave me this beautiful cookbook, and since my idea of cooking is turning on the microwave, I thought you would do it more justice than I would."

BONUS POINTS

You're a bit short of money to spend on presents this year. Who says you have to purchase gifts? Sometimes a "coupon" for a home-cooked favorite meal, a backrub, or a dog-walking date can be a huge plus. Just write out your coupon, and make it amusing to the receiver. Hint: baby boomers are especially grateful for tech help from the younger set. Perhaps a lesson in how to navigate Facebook?

Declining Gifts

There are times when accepting a gift isn't appropriate. Most often, this happens in situations involving expensive items. For example, a client might give a service provider an expensive fountain pen or jewelry, or someone in a new relationship might give a pricey bauble. Handle such a situation by saying, "Much as I appreciate your thinking of me this way, I really can't accept your kind gift. It's far too generous. Please know that I do thank you, though." If you happen to work for a company whose policies prohibit accepting gifts, go ahead and cite the company policy, while letting the giver know that you appreciate his thoughtfulness.

E-Gifting, Registries, Gift Cards, and Gift Certificates

Before you place the order for a gift, decide whether to have the gift sent to you (which will allow you to wrap and personalize it), or if you'd rather send it directly to the recipient. If you choose the latter, find a reputable, reliable e-tailer, one you have used previously or that friends have recommended. It's hard to go wrong shopping online at household names like Tiffany & Co., Brooks Brothers, Crate & Barrel, Zappos, Amazon, Barnes & Noble, L.L.Bean, Williams-Sonoma, or MuseumShop.com.

If you decide to have the retailer send the item, request that it be gift wrapped. Once you've ordered your gift selection, send a card or note telling the recipient that something is on its way. If you're the recipient, call or email right away to say thank you and to let the person know the gift has arrived. You must then follow up with a thank-you note.

When you know a person's interests, gift cards and gift certificates are always welcome. Some of the most popular items are gift certificates for restaurants, coffee shops, bookstores, and movie theaters. Personalize your gift with a note letting the person know that you "hope they'll enjoy a dinner on the town," for example. If you purchased the gift card at a third-party vendor, such as a grocery store, include the gift receipt to ensure that activating the gift card will be smooth.

Registries are a mixed blessing. For one thing, a registry never should be listed on a wedding invitation or on a housewarming party invitation. When you're invited to a wedding, it's fair to ask the person you know in the wedding party if the couple is registered anywhere. It's also fair for you to have a wish list, provided you only share it with your nearest and dearest with whom you already exchange gifts. Listing a gift registry on a bridal shower or baby shower invitation is acceptable, because the main function of those occasions is gift giving to provide a foundation for the new chapter in the mom's or the bride's life.

Having said that, registries are practical when people don't know you well or live at a distance. In an effort to make already easy things easier, here are some suggestions:

- Register in only one or two stores that are readily reached by telephone and online.
- List things you really need and that are not over the moon in terms of cost.
- List a few larger items so that a few friends might contribute to a single gift.

Registering in a dozen places for exclusively high-end merchandise makes you look like a greedy, spoiled brat.

Hostess Gifts

Beware of bringing gifts that require immediate attention from a host who may be frantically busy in the kitchen, or have limited space. Cut flowers, for example, require the host to stop what he's doing, find a vase, add water, and then position the bouquet in a place of honor.

Instead, try an easy-care plant, chocolates, or a bottle of wine "to put away for later." That relieves the host of the pressure of having to deal with the gift immediately.

Another lovely option is to send flowers the day after the party. Or, if your host has a pet, both the pet and its guardian will appreciate your gift of some pet treats.

Surprise Gifts

If somebody gives you something unexpectedly, you might immediately feel that you need to reciprocate. But very little, if anything, is kind or gracious about a "knee-jerk" gift.

This seems to happen most embarrassingly at holiday season. Should someone take you by surprise with a gift, simply smile and say, "Thank you so much. What a lovely surprise! You made my day." Down the road, should you happen on something that reminds you of the giver, go ahead and present it with as much affection as the surprise gift you received. The gift you give as a surprise—when there's no reason for it—is the best gift of all.

You just might receive a beautiful pot of violets in February, with a note that reads, "Just thought that some violets in the snow would bring you a smile." It will become one of your most cherished memories.

On the other hand, if you simply can't resist repaying a kindness immediately, you might consider keeping a supply of generic gifts for just this purpose. Coasters, cocktail napkins, chocolates, note cards, and wine all work well when you're caught off guard. Just take care that your gift is something the other person really might use.

Holiday Tipping

The holiday season is a good time to show anyone who's part of the fabric of your everyday life how much you appreciate them. Think of them as part of your team. Your team might include doormen, housecleaners, babysitters, tutors, personal trainers, hairdressers, manicurists, massage therapists, dog walkers, and delivery people.

Some general principles apply. Consider your own personal resources and your ability to be generous during the holiday season. When you're in a position to be especially generous, do so. It will come back to you later, and make up for a downturn should you have one.

Consider, too, the section of the country where you live. Standards for the Midwest are different from the East Coast or West Coast, where the cost of living is much higher. What kind of place does the person being tipped work in? Are we talking luxury spa setting or modest storefront nail salon? How long has the person you're tipping been part of your team? How long have you been parking your car at that garage?

Give the equivalent of one week's service for each year worked, whenever you can. For example, if someone walks your dog once a week, then tip the amount of one walk. If he walks the dog five days a week, then tip the equivalent of five walks. This guideline applies when someone has been providing you with a service for six months or more. When someone is new to the job, your tip can be more modest.

Make sure that you include a note with each envelope. You might say something like, "This is to let you know how much I appreciate all the times you took Zsa Zsa out for a walk and a romp, even in bad weather. And I thank you for bringing her back without muddy paws. Happy holidays!"

It's an especially nice idea to distribute your holiday tips as Thanksgiving gifts if you live in the United States. For one thing, it's a uniquely North American holiday. For another, your gift won't get lost in the holiday chaos, and thus it will be more distinct. Short on funds for holiday tips? Save up your dough and surprise everyone with a Valentine's Day tip.

Don't tip professionals such as doctors, lawyers, nurses, or teachers. However, a little goodwill goes a long way, so once you've checked the policies, feel free to give something modest and thoughtful—as long as you include a note. For instance, if you know your child's teacher is an avid moviegoer, a gift card for two movie passes would be appreciated.

Private clubs generally don't permit tipping of employees. If you belong to a club, or you use one, make a contribution to the holiday fund.

Resources

The following resources were consulted during the writing of this book.

General Reference

Baldrige, Letitia. *Letitia Baldrige's New Manners for New Times.* New York: Scribner, 2003.

Mitchell, Mary. *The Complete Idiots' Guide to Etiquette, Third Edition.* New York: Alpha Books, 2004.

Chapter 1

Mitchell, Mary. *The First Five Minutes.* New York: John Wiley and Sons, Inc., 1998.

Chapter 3

KidsHealth.org

Chapter 5

Mitchell, Mary. *Class Acts.* Rowman and Littlefield, 2003.

Chapter 6

In General:

geekwire.com, especially articles by Frank Catalano

Emails and Texting:

Baude, Dawn-Michelle, PhD. *The Executive Guide to E-mail Correspondence*. Franklin Lakes, NJ: The Career Press, Inc., 2007.

Shipley, David, and Will Schwalbe. *Send*. New York: Alfred A. Knopf, 2007.

Social Networking:

"3 reasons to try social media add-ons for Outlook or Gmail," Bruce2b.com

"How recruiters use social networks to screen candidates," mashable.com/2011/10/23/how-recruiters-use-social-networks-to-screen-candidates-infographic/

Statistics on Social Media, socialmediaexaminer.com/5-social-media-tips-for-finding-and-engaging-your-target-audience-new-research/

Chapter 11

KidsHealth.org

Maloff, Chalda, PhD, and Susan MacDuff Wood, MA. *Business and Social Etiquette with Disabled People*. Springfield, IL: Charles C. Thomas, 1988.

Chapter 12

Toussaint, David. *The Gay Couple's Guide to Wedding Planning*. South Portland, ME: Sellers Publishing, Inc., 2012.

Index

F

G

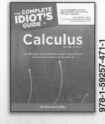
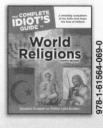

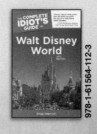